Brimming with creative inspiration, how-to projects, and useful information to enrich your everyday life, Quarto Knows is a favorite destination for those pursuing their interests and passions. Visit our site and dig deeper with our books into your area of interest: Quarto Creates, Quarto Cooks, Quarto Homes, Quarto Lives, Quarto Drives, Quarto Explores, Quarto Gifts, or Quarto Kids.

First Published in 2021 by The Harvard Common Press, an imprint of The Quarto Group,
100 Cummings Center, Suite 265-D,
Beverly, MA 01915, USA.
T (978) 282-9590 F (978) 283-2742 QuartoKnows.com

The Harvard Common Press titles are also available at discount for retail, wholesale, promotional, and bulk purchase. For details, contact the Special Sales Manager by email at specialsales@quarto.com or by mail at The Quarto Group, Attn: Special Sales Manager, 100 Cummings Center, Suite 265-D, Beverly, MA 01915, USA.

25 24 23 22 21   1 2 3 4 5

ISBN: 978-0-76037-159-6

Digital edition published in 2021
eISBN: 978-0-7603-7160-2

Library of Congress Cataloging-in-Publication Data

Names: Callaway, Hayley, author.
Title: Sweet talk cookies / Hayley Callaway.
Description: Beverly, MA : The Harvard Common Press, 2021. | Includes
  index. | Summary: „In Sweet Talk Cookies, you'll find dozens of sweet
  but sassy cookie designs with customizable messages from Instagram star
  Hayley Cakes and Cookies"-- Provided by publisher.
Identifiers: LCCN 2021031181 (print) | LCCN 2021031182 (ebook) | ISBN
  9780760371596 | ISBN 9780760371602 (ebook)
Subjects: LCSH: Cookies. | Baking. | LCGFT: Cookbooks.
Classification: LCC TX772 .C355 2021 (print) | LCC TX772 (ebook) | DDC
  641.86/54--dc23
LC record available at https://lccn.loc.gov/2021031181
LC ebook record available at https://lccn.loc.gov/2021031182

Design and layout: Debbie Berne
Photography: Kimberly Davis, kimberlydavisphotography.com;
except page 190: Hayden and Jamye Callaway

Printed in China

CREATIVE DESIGNS FOR BIRTHDAYS, HOLIDAYS, AND EVERY DAY

Sweet Talk COOKIES

HAYLEY CALLAWAY
AKA THEHAYLEYCAKES

HARVARD
COMMON
PRESS

Contents

The Basics

Basic Cookie Techniques

There are three basic steps to decorating cookies: the outline, the flood, and the top decorations (top deco). Here are tips for each part to help you translate the tutorials onto any cookie design!

The Outline

This step is always done with a thicker consistency, royal icing. I refer to it throughout this book as detail icing or detail royal icing. The outline serves as a dam and will hold in the thinner flood icing (aka glaze icing).

The outline is super important to get right—and clean—because it determines the shape of your design. Make sure your outline stays on top of the cookie. If you run the outline off the edge of the cookie, the flood icing will have nothing to hold it in place. This can cause runoff. It isn't the end of the world, but it will make for a messy-looking cookie for sure!

I use a PME Supatubes No. 2 Writer tip for all outlining. This creates a line that is thick enough to hold the icing in, but not so thick that you can blatantly see the outline when the design is finished.

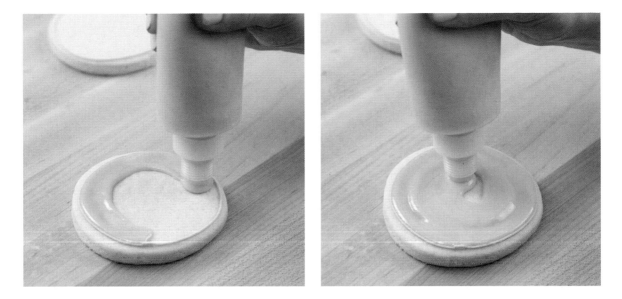

Flooding

Think of this as basically coloring in the lines—just on cookies! Usually, you will flood the cookie in whatever color you outlined it in, but that is not a hard-and-fast rule, especially if you want a black outline to make the cookie look more cartoon-y.

Your flood icing needs to be thin enough to spread itself out and touch the edge of the outline. You also want it thin so that it will make itself smooth without you having to do a lot of work. If it is too thick, it may leave holes.

You want the flood icing to stay within the boundaries of the outline. If your icing is too thin and does run over the outline, let it dry and set up. To do damage control, use a toothpick or a small knife to scrape the excess off.

For smaller spaces, flood using a smaller tip for added control and precision. Be aware that this can be time-consuming. When you are just starting, using smaller tips can also help you avoid running over the edge. I usually will not flood with anything smaller than a number 8 tip, for the sake of time.

When flooding a larger cookie or a solid color, you may want to use your bottle without a tip. This actually helps create a thinner coat of flood icing. You can use a toothpick to push the flood into a tiny corner or to reach the edge of the outline, if needed.

We don't recommend flooding using piping bags. You can do it by tying off the top of the bag, but it's messier and you'll have less control over the thin flood icing. Get yourself some bottles—you deserve it!

Glaze vs. Royal Icing Flood

For this book, we are teaching you *our* way of decorating, using two different icings. We outline and top deco with royal icing because it dries hard—with a crunch. It is perfect for piping intricate details. We prefer an icing to cover the cookie with a softer bite and sweeter taste. That is why we make a separate recipe for the flood.

If you choose not to do this, you can flood using royal icing and thin it out. Just remember that this leaves room for making the flood too thick or too thin. If you make the glaze according to our recipe, you don't have to worry about consistency for flood: it will turn out right every time.

Wet on Wet

Wet on wet is one technique that you will want to learn and practice. This is simply a design that is done on the cookie while the flood icing is still wet. It allows the design to lie completely flat into the background, making it easy to write or decorate on top of it after it dries (for example by adding polka dots). Use small tips for these wet-on-wet designs; I recommend sticking with the PME 2 tips.

When flooding the initial solid color for a wet-on-wet cookie, keep it thin so that when you add the second round of colors on top (the polka dots), it does not force the flood to overflow the edge. If you are using a wet-on-wet design and it runs over, there is little hope for a fix, unless you can alter your top deco designs to cover up the parts that ran off.

You can also accomplish the wet-on-wet technique by using the glaze flood, and then while that is still wet, using your detail royal icing to do even more detailed designs. I recommend using this combination of icings to get colored stripes in the background, chevron, or swirly filigree. Simply flood the solid color background, then use your detail icing to pipe your design on top while it is still wet, allowing it to sink into the wet glaze.

For top details that you *don't* want to sink in, always let your flood icing set up before you move on to the top deco designs. If the background glaze is dry, it creates an easier surface to write on. It's also easier to work with because if you drag the tip across the dry surface, it won't create a hole in the icing.

When flooding, you may notice you see a few air bubbles coming up. Pop these with a little toothpick while your icing is still wet and you are good to go!

Top Decoration

This is where the cookie magic usually happens! This step is done using royal icing. It holds its shape well and allows you to pipe intricate details that hold their shape. If you try to do this with glaze, it will run everywhere . . . I do not recommend it!

For the consistency, aim for something like peanut butter: thick, but spreadable. You want it to hold a peak if you run a knife down to the bottom and back up! This should give you a consistency that allows you to squeeze the bag without it hurting your hand, but it isn't so thin that the shape doesn't hold up.

Supplies

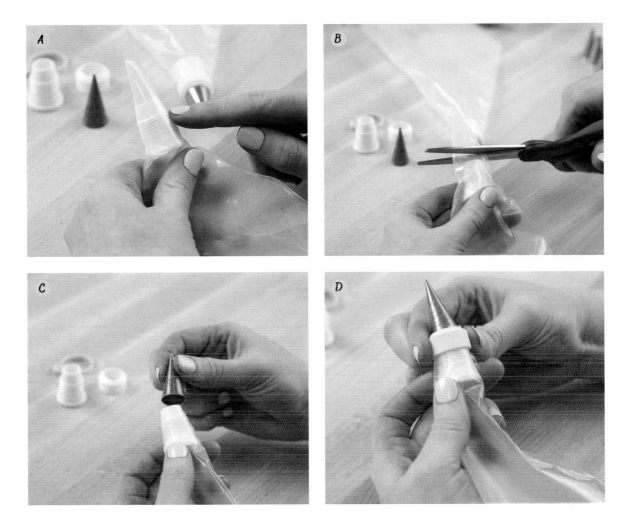

You may be a little worried when you look at all these fancy cookies, thinking you need to invest in a whole lot of tools and materials—but that is not true! Sure, you could, but I'm here to show you the easiest way to do things. There are a few *key* items you can't live without as a cookie decorator. Add the rest you can to your collection as you go!

Pastry Bags

I recommend disposable piping bags from Kee-seal. If you use our icing "pod" method (page 24), rinse them after use and reuse them. They hold up well, which is important! I don't recommend "tipless piping bags." They are super cheap, but they burst easily. I also find you have better control over your icing if you use a tip, especially when writing.

Couplers

If you use Kee-seal pastry bags or sturdier disposable bags, such as Wilton, fit them with a coupler. Fit every bag you use with one of these, as it allows you to change tip sizes easily on the same bag of color.

A coupler has two pieces: the main coupler and the screw collar. To fit a coupler, drop the coupler into the bag, lightly press it into the plastic to leave an indentation right where the screw rings begin. *See A.* Loosen the coupler piece and cut on the indented line it left on the bag. *See B.* Drop a pod of icing in, cut the extra plastic wrap, and screw on the piping tip! *See C and D.*

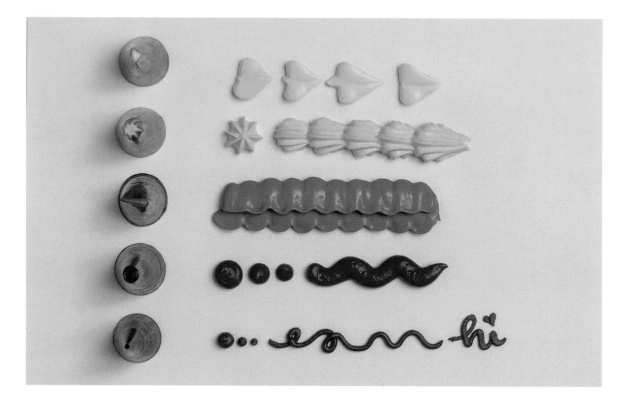

Metal Piping Tips

The PME Supatubes No. 2 Writer is a must-have. Yes, seriously. You can do almost anything you need to with that tip. They are more expensive than the standard number 2, but the PME tips do not have a seam where the metal is joined, so your icing will not curl as you pipe it. Instead, it will come out in a perfectly straight line. Trust me on this, you will have so much control over what you are writing or piping!

For the recipes in this book, use the tip you feel most comfortable with. The smaller the tip you use on your flood bottles, the slower the icing will come out and the smaller spaces you can fit the tip into. I recommend using a tip number 5 to a tip number 12 when flooding smaller spaces.

Leaf tips are good for 3-dimensional, realistic leaves. When using this tip, hold the bag where the V-shapes are on the side. Squeeze and then gently release while you stop squeezing. This tip is also good for 3-D succulents with a spiky texture.

Star tips are perfect for piping a little swirl flower, succulents, or a cool textured border around the edge of a cookie.

Squeeze Bottles

Flood icing runs right out the back end of a bag when you lay it flat! That's why I *love* using bottles. It can be tricky to pour the icing into the bottle: go slow and get a thin stream of icing flowing. It will save you a lot of trouble in the long run!

These bottles come with a plastic tip attached. ***See A.*** I keep the screw collar, but usually throw the plastic tip away. They are flimsy and don't let the icing come out cleanly. When flooding a large surface, you don't need a tip; it will only take you more time. If the space you are trying to flood is smaller than the opening of the bottle, I recommend using metal piping tips. Try a tip 10 or smaller.

Food Coloring

I only use gel food coloring. There are many brands out there, and all are of similar quality. Look for AmeriColor, Chefmaster colors, and Wilton colors. You can find them at your local craft stores. I do ***not*** recommend using liquid food coloring you can buy in droppers at the grocery store. This can alter the consistency of your icing and does not produce the vibrant colors we are going for! ***See B and C.***

Don't be afraid to mix up your gel colors to get a unique custom color. I like to add a hint of peach to my pinks, just to change the tone. For more on color mixing, see page 26.

Edible Glitter

Sometimes called "tinker dust" or "disco dust," this is a food-grade glitter to make your cookies sparkle! It can be a cute touch, but use this stuff sparingly because you don't want to taste or feel the texture of the glitter when you bite into the cookie.

Sprinkles

I don't care what anyone tells you . . . you can *never* have too many sprinkles. You can find sprinkle mixes almost anywhere, and some are super fancy. We have a bunch of awesome mixes available on our website: hayleycakesandcookies.com.

Gold and Silver Luster Dust

Use a tiny dropper or one of your squeeze bottles to mix the dust with a clear alcohol; we usually use vodka because it has the least taste. The alcohol will evaporate out, leaving only the metallic dust on the cookie. To avoid the alcohol, use clear vanilla extract. It may take longer to dry, but it will do the job. *See A.*

Parchment Paper

Parchment is great for sketching designs and using them as a cookie cutter template directly on top of your dough. I recommend baking all of your cookies on parchment paper. It means less cleaning for you and your cookie sheets. And the cookies turn out better, with fewer brown edges, which is what we want.

Plastic Wrap

We use plastic cling wrap to make our icing pods. Yes, you could skip this step and put the icing directly into the piping bags. But you will likely want to reuse your piping bags, and this will save you some cleanup! You will need plastic wrap to make the unicorn poo/rainbow icing (page 28).

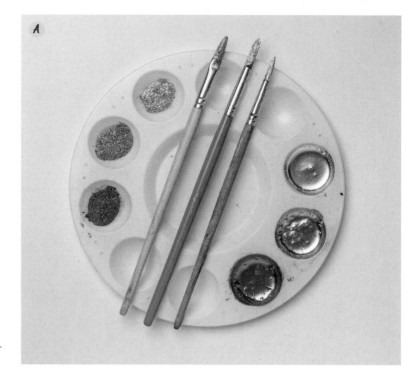

A

Toothpicks

Nothing fancy here! Some people may sell you on a "scribe tool" to move your icing around, but who wants to wash that every time? I love toothpicks for popping air bubbles and pushing icing into tight corners.

Tips for Using Luster Dust

Add the alcohol a little at a time to make an edible paint with the luster dust.

Avoid adding too much alcohol so that the gold/silver stays vibrant.

Use food-safe paintbrushes to brush onto dry icing.

You can also brush on wet icing, if you are very gentle. Be careful: you run a greater risk of the icing moving or messing up when you touch it while it is wet.

When painting something silver, I pipe it in gray. If I am using gold, I pipe that detail in ivory. That way if I miss a spot painting, it will be less noticeable.

Food Pen

Food pen is the greatest thing to ever happen for writing small or adding a little face on a cookie! Make sure the cookie is completely dry before you use food pen. Use very gentle pressure, so you don't poke a hole in the icing.

Food pens come in many colors, but black is my main go-to! I use the FooDoodler for fine-tip writing and details. I also love the felt-tip food pens for thicker lines or stripes, as it creates a bolder look. *See B.*

Cookie Cutters

Last but not least, you can amass a *huge* collection of cookie cutters—and you don't even have to try hard! A few of my favorite online sellers are KaleidaCuts, Sheyb Designs, That's a Nice Cookie Cutter, Sweetleigh Printed . . . and that is only naming a few! I love browsing these sites and Etsy, because new releases can inspire me to come up with new cookie designs!

You can also try hand-cutting a design! This is how I used to make *all* of my cookies, because you just couldn't find any unique shapes. If you don't want to buy a cookie cutter or have a small quantity for a custom shape, you can simply draw the shape (or print it out) on a piece of paper. Then cut it out, lay it on top of the cookie dough, and use a small paring knife to cut around the edge of your paper template. If you are cutting more than a couple dozen, you can also inquire with a shop about getting a custom-printed shape,

as many are happy to help you! *See C.*

Small Bowls

I like to use a bowl that holds 12 to 16 ounces (355 to 474 ml) for mixing colors. This is enough icing for one bag of color, and the bowl fits nicely in the palm of your hand while stirring!

Small Spatulas

I like to use flexible spatulas. They scrape down all areas of the bowl to make sure your color is fully mixed in!

The OG Sugar Cookie Recipe

The one that started it all. The big whammy. THE. BEST. COOKIES. EVER. Whatever you want to call them, this roll-out sugar cookie recipe is a game changer with a secret ingredient that makes all the difference. These are soft, dense, and DELICIOUS. Plus, with a few modifications, you can change up the flavor to anything you want!

In a large bowl, whisk together the flour, baking powder, and salt. Set aside.

In the bowl of your stand mixer or with an electric hand mixer, cream the butter and sugar for about 2 minutes, until light and fluffy. Add the eggs and mix until incorporated. Scrape down the sides of the bowl. Add the vanilla, almond extract (if using), and cream cheese. Mix until combined. Scrape down the sides of the bowl again.

Add in the dry ingredients in 2 to 3 batches, so you don't send your flour flying! Mix on low speed, until just incorporated. Do not overmix the dough once the dry ingredients are added; this will create a tough and crumbly cookie, and we don't want that!

Once the dough has come together, turn the dough out onto a piece of plastic wrap. Wrap tightly and refrigerate for at least 4 hours before using. (It will last up to 2 weeks in the refrigerator.)

Roll the dough out onto your floured surface, ¼ inch (6 mm) thick. Preheat your oven to 350°F (180°C, or gas mark 4) and cut out your desired shapes. Bake for 8 to 10 minutes. Take a look at the cookies. They should have a slight crispiness and light brown color around the edge—but they should still be very light in color! If you like a crispier cookie, try baking for 12 to 14 minutes.

Lemon Rolled Sugar Cookies: Omit the almond extract. Add 1 tablespoon (6 g) fresh lemon zest and 1 teaspoon lemon extract.

Megafetti Rolled Sugar Cookies: Sprinkles make EVERYTHING better. Try adding ½ cup (96 g) of assorted sprinkles to your dough for a fun rainbow flair!

6½ cups (27.5 oz/780 g) all-purpose flour	2 eggs
2 teaspoons (9 g) baking powder	1 tablespoon (15 ml) vanilla extract
1 teaspoon salt	1 teaspoon almond extract (optional)
1 lb. (455 g) butter	4 oz (115 g) cream cheese
2 cups (14.1 oz/400 g) sugar	

Yield: Dough to make about 20 cookies

Almond Wedding Rolled Sugar Cookies: Add 1 full tablespoon (15 ml) of almond extract in addition to 1 tablespoon (15 ml) of vanilla. Almond lovers get it.

Gluten-free Rolled Sugar Cookies: This recipe works perfectly when substituting a gluten-free flour blend in place of the traditional all-purpose flour. Our favorite is Cup 4 Cup brand, which substitutes just like its name says, cup for cup! I like to use an additional teaspoon of vanilla when making gluten-free cookies, because I feel that gluten-free flour masks the flavoring a bit.

Strawberry Rolled Sugar Cookies: Okay, this may sound weird, but trust me, it is delicious. Add one small package (3 ounces, or 85 g) of strawberry Jell-O when you add the dry ingredients. And yes, this will work with ANY Jell-O flavoring. Sounds crazy, but it doesn't change the texture if you don't overmix, and it lends the brightest flavor to your cookies!

Gingerbread Cut-out Cookies

This recipe is soft and chewy, and it's the perfect way to spice up your holiday cookie designs!

Cream the butter, molasses, and brown sugar together in your electric stand mixer, until light and fluffy. Add in the egg and mix until incorporated. Scrape down the sides and bottom of the bowl.

In a separate bowl, combine the salt, cinnamon, ginger, cloves, flour, baking powder, and baking soda. Stir these dry ingredients together, then add the dry mix in 2 to 3 batches into your creamed butter mixture. Make sure not to overmix! When you add the flour to your recipe, mix just until the flour is mixed into the dough.

Once the dough has come together, turn the dough out onto a piece of plastic wrap. Wrap tightly and refrigerate for at least 2 hours before using. Note that if this dough is not refrigerated long enough it will be super sticky and hard to cut out! (It will last up to 2 weeks in the refrigerator.)

Roll the dough out onto your floured surface, ¼ inch (6 mm) thick. Preheat your oven to 350°F

1 cup (8 oz/225 g) unsalted butter	2 teaspoons (5 g) cinnamon
1 cup (235 ml) molasses	2 teaspoons (4 g) ginger
1 cup (225 g) packed brown sugar (I prefer dark, but light brown will work!)	¼ teaspoon cloves
	4 cups (500 g) all-purpose flour
1 egg	1 teaspoon baking powder
1 teaspoon salt	½ teaspoon baking soda

Yield: Dough to make about 20 cookies

(180°C, or gas mark 4) and cut out your desired shapes. Bake for 8 to 10 minutes. If you like a crispier cookie, try baking for 12 to 14 minutes.

Tips for rolling dough

When your dough is chilled, lightly flour your work surface. Be careful not to add too much flour; this will incorporate into your dough and could make your cookies dry.

Some people swear by rolling out cookies in powdered sugar. It does make for a tasty addition, but give the tops of the cookie a weird texture when decorating. It is worth trying one day when you have the time!

Be careful not to roll out the same ball of dough too many times—the dough will toughen. I like to roll out half of the ball of dough on my floured surface, with a light sprinkling of flour on top of the dough to prevent the rolling pin from sticking. Once I have cut all the cookies I can from the initial roll out, I lightly ball the dough back up, and start with the other untouched ball of dough

and do the same. When both balls of dough have been used and re-balled, I combine them, to limit the re-rolls.

I like to roll my dough ¼ inch (6 mm) thick. There are specialty rolling pins you can order to keep your dough the same thickness throughout. Or you can just eyeball it, trying to keep it the same thickness throughout your slab.

Chocolate Cut-out Cookies

These cookies are rich and chocolaty, but they also make a cool contrast between a lighter-colored icing design! Keep these in mind when you want something to really pop on a cookie!

Cream the butter and both sugars together in your electric stand mixer, until light and fluffy. Add the eggs, one at a time, and scrape down the sides of the bowl. Add in the vanilla and cream cheese, and beat until combined.

In a separate bowl, whisk together the cocoa, flour, baking powder, and salt. In 2 to 3 additions, add it to the butter mixture, being careful not to overmix. Mix just until incorporated into the dough. Scrape down the sides of the bowl and do a quick mix one more time.

Once the dough has come together, divide the dough into two roughly equal-sized balls and turn the dough out onto a piece of plastic wrap. Wrap tightly and refrigerate for at least 2 hours before using. (It will last up to 2 weeks in the refrigerator.)

Roll the dough out onto your floured surface, ¼ inch (6 mm) thick. Preheat your oven to 350°F (180°C, or gas mark 4) and cut out your desired shapes. Bake for 8 to 10 minutes. If you like a crispier cookie, try baking for 12 to 14 minutes.

Variation: For a fan favorite, add in 1 to 2 cups (90 to 180 g) of peanut butter chips for a chocolate–peanut butter cookie flavor!

1 lb. (455 g) butter
1 cup (200 g) sugar
1 cup (225 g) packed light brown sugar
2 eggs
1 tablespoon (15 ml) vanilla extract
4 oz (115 g) cream cheese
1 cup (86 g) cocoa powder
6 cups (27.5 oz/800 g) all-purpose flour
2 teaspoons (9 g) baking powder
1 teaspoon salt

Yield: Dough to make about 20 cookies

Royal Icing
(aka Decorator's Icing or Detail Icing)

This is the recipe to use for the "detail icing" mentioned in the cookie designs. It is thick, holds its shape, and dries hard and crunchy. Royal icing is perfect for writing, outlining, and piping any details onto the top of your cookie. Most cookie decorators use this icing to frost the entire cookie. We use a glaze frosting (page 30) for the largest area of the icing, because it dries softer and sweeter. And this is why we think our cookies taste the best!

Measure the clear vanilla into your measuring cup. Then add warm water up to the 1½-cup (355 ml) line. Pour the water-vanilla mixture and meringue powder into the bowl of your stand mixer. Mix on speed 3 (medium-low) for 1 minute, until frothy and the powder dissolves.

Add the sifted powdered sugar and mix on medium-low until combined, then scrape down the sides of the bowl well. Turn the speed of the mixer up to speed 7 (medium-high) and whip for 3 minutes. The icing should be very thick, holding stiff peaks.

To add a little extra shine to your royal icing, add the light corn syrup. Stir it in using low speed on the mixer.

2 tablespoons (28 ml) clear vanilla extract or flavoring of your choice	4 lb. (1.8 kg) powdered sugar, sifted
1¼ cups minus 2 tablespoons (267 ml) warm water	¼ cup (60 ml) light corn syrup (optional)
⅔ cup, plus 3 teaspoons (105 g) meringue powder or powdered egg whites	**SUPPLIES** Electric stand mixer

Yield: Makes about 6 cups (1.2 kg), enough for detail work on four to five 20-cookie batches, plus leftovers.

Notes

* Royal icing will keep in the fridge for three weeks or in the freezer for six months. Whip in mixer again when ready to use.

* Make sure the water is warm. Don't always be in a rush like me. Be Goldilocks on this . . . make sure it's not hot, but not cold. Get it juuuuust right.

* I recommend using at least 1 tablespoon (15 ml) of vanilla and 1 tablespoon (15 ml) of another flavoring (if not making vanilla). Orange flavoring, hazelnut, and almond are great options. Lemon flavoring works for a tart lemon icing, but with citrus flavors avoid using zest. Anything "chunky" could ruin the smooth and sleek look of the professional-level cookies you are about to decorate!!

Royal Icing Consistencies

You do not want to use an icing this thick in a piping bag as it will break your hand for sure! Thin out the icing while it is on the mixer using small amounts of water at a time, or transfer this thick royal icing into an airtight storage container and thin out each bag of icing as you mix your colors.

I prefer to do it bowl by bowl because it is a lot harder to make the icing too thin. If you try to thin out the entire batch on the mixer, you may over-water it, and there is not much you can do to get it thicker once you add too much water!

When thinning out your royal icing for detail and outline consistency, *make sure it still holds its shape!* You just want it to be a little smoother and shinier before you put it into your plastic wrap pod, and then into your piping bag, so it is easier on your hands to pipe.

To flood your cookie with royal icing, and not make a separate glaze recipe, continue adding water to your royal icing until it reaches a thick shampoo-like consistency. This means when you run a knife through the icing, the icing will close back up and smooth itself out after about 15 seconds. If the line from the knife never closes back up, it is too thick for flooding. If it closes back up superfast, your icing may be too thin and will run over the edge of the cookie, overflowing the outline, and you don't want that!

Note: Perfecting royal icing consistency is one of the biggest problems that cookie decorators have. This is why I stand firm that using glaze to flood is a time-saver, not to mention the best-tasting option! If you are having any problems with the royal icing recipe or consistencies, check out our website and YouTube channel where we have a video tutorial posted to help you troubleshoot! See Resources on page 185.

See Resources on page 185.

Troubleshooting Tips for Royal Icing

＊The icing seems too loose and isn't holding a peak after 3 minutes.
You may need to mix it a little longer to whip up that meringue powder! Be careful: You don't want to overmix; this will cause other problems.

＊The icing is crumbling when it is dry.
You may have overmixed your icing. Getting *too much* air into the frosting can make it crumbly in texture for the final product. Find the exact time it takes for your icing to reach stiff peak consistency, then stick to that time precisely!

Another reason for crumbly icing could be too much food coloring. You can achieve a deep icing color by letting your frosting "develop" for an hour or two after coloring it.

＊The icing falls or is not drying.
Avoid any oil at all costs! Oil, butter, etc., are the enemy of royal icing. Oil can make the icing fall or not dry properly if it comes in contact—yes, that means even a little residue. If you have any issues, wipe down your entire bowl and mixer blade with lemon juice or white vinegar to get rid of any oily residue.

How to Prepare Royal Icing in Piping Bags (The Pod Method)

Stir up the color you want (see page 26), then fold open your piping bag and place the icing directly into the bag. Close off the bag somehow so air is not freely flowing into the icing, because it will dry and crust up. We use elastic bag ties to keep the top of the bag closed while squeezing or while the bag is lying on the counter. **See A.**

For our pod method: Simply lay out a square of plastic wrap and place a plop of icing in the center of the square. Fold one corner diagonally across to the other corner. Then roll the icing up to meet the corner. From here, grab both long ends of the plastic wrap and spin it as if you are about to pop someone with a wet towel. Yes, for real. I know you know what I mean. **See B, C, D.**

Take your piping bag and insert the inner piece of the coupler. Cut off the tip of the plastic bag, right where the lines of the screw begin. Place the pod inside, pulling the tail of the plastic wrap through the end as it comes out of the coupler. *See E, F.*

As soon as you can see icing peeking through the end of the coupler, snip off that long plastic tail with scissors. *See G.* Then place the piping tip and plastic screw collar onto the bag, over the inner coupler, and voilà! *See H.* Use the elastic bag tie to twist off the top of the piping bag and you are ready to go. *See I.*

I like to keep all my icing colors standing up in a bin I found at the container store. It is just a clear plastic, rectangular bin, that keeps the bags standing up. I place a damp towel in the bottom of the bin to prevent the icing from drying in the tips as they sit out.

Storing Royal Icing

If you're not using it right away, make sure your batch of royal icing is stored in an airtight container. You can leave it on the counter or store it in the refrigerator. Before using it, stir it back together as it may have separated. Alternatively, place it all back in the stand mixer for a quick whip, for the best results.

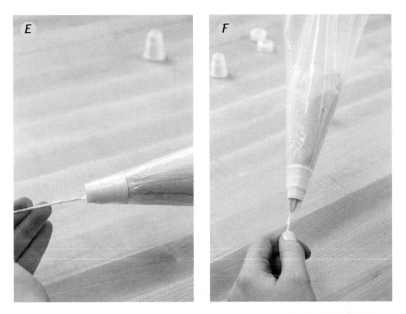

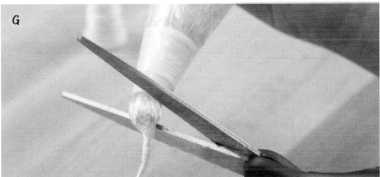

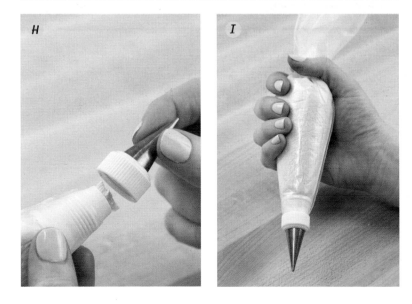

Color Mixing
for Royal Icing/Detail Icing

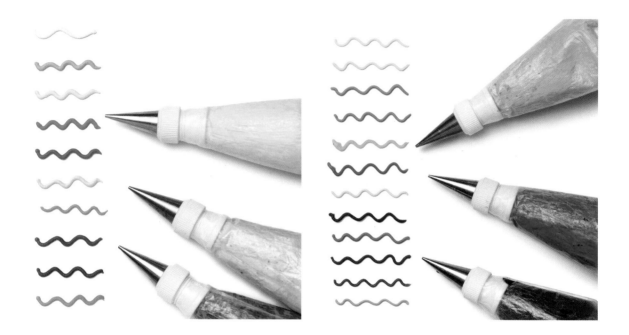

I recommend certain colors for many of the cookies in this book, but be creative and make these your own: go lighter or darker, mix and match. Please don't get tied down to using the food coloring exactly as it comes out of the bottle. Some of the most beautiful hues are made when you mix two colors together!

Color Tips

If you add too much food coloring, your icing will dry crumbly and will be *super* delicate. This won't be too big of a problem unless you are planning to ship your cookies (they will be ruined in transit).

Royal icing colors sit for a few hours after you mix, and the color develops into a deeper, darker shade. This is especially true for reds and blacks. I often err on the side of a little bit lighter than I want the color to be when dry.

To mix colors, I use a small mixing bowl and small flat spatulas. Place a heaping scoop of icing— about ½ cup (63 g) is good to fill one piping bag. Squirt your food coloring into the bowl. Add about ½ teaspoon of water and stir. Continue adding water a teaspoon at a time, until the consistency is smooth. The icing

should look a bit glossy, but still holds a peak.

When mixing multiple colors, you can start with related colors and move from light to dark. That way you can use the same bowl to mix all the colors and not have to wash between each color. For example, mix yellow before mixing orange. Move on to red, then dark pink. You can try moving the other way, to light pink, using the residual dark pink icing in the bowl. When you add more white royal icing to the bowl, it will turn to a lovely shade of light pink!

To create an ombre array of colors, start with the darkest shade first. Mix that color completely. When you go to make that pod of icing, leave half of the colored icing in the bowl. Add more white royal icing and stir it up, creating a lighter shade. As you pod each color, leave less and less of the previous color in the bowl, making each new bag of icing lighter, without having to add different amounts of food coloring!

Notice that in our glaze icing (page 30) we add a white food coloring to make the color vibrant. I do not recommend ever adding white food coloring to royal icing. It can mess up the consistency of your icing. Plus, the royal icing is stark white to begin with and needs no white food coloring.

Here is a color chart on our favorites! This is also a list in the order we mix them in, so we use only one bowl from start to finish on the warm colors, and one bowl for the cool colors! We use AmeriColor gel food coloring, but any gel food coloring will work. These names are associated with AmeriColor, and most other food coloring brands have similar hues:

Warm Colors

· **White**
· **Ivory**
· **Yellow: equal parts electric yellow and egg yellow**
· **Electric orange**

· **Dark pink: electric pink and small drop of orange** *Add orange to change the electric pink to a less neon vibe and a more classic hot pink color. Add more orange to create a salmon/coral color.*
· **Light pink** *I rarely add any food coloring. I just use the residual icing from the hot pink bowl. If starting from scratch and only making light pink, try using deep pink and a drop of peach.*
· **Peach**
· **Red/super red**
· **Dark purple: equal parts electric purple and regal purple**
· **Light purple** *I mix this the same as the light pink, based off of the residual from dark purple. If starting from scratch, just use small amounts of both electric purple and regal purple.*

Cool Colors

· **Mint: mostly turquoise and a drop or two of electric green** *Experiment by adding green for a spearmint shade or more turquoise for more of a wintery/blue mint color.*
· **Lime green/electric green**
· **Dark green/leaf green**
· **Dark turquoise**
· **Light turquoise** *Use the residual icing from the dark turquoise or use small amounts of turquoise food coloring.*
· **Royal blue**
· **Baby blue** *Use the residual icing from the royal blue you made or add small drops of royal blue coloring.*

· **Black** *Make sure not to go too dark with the black. Aim for a dark gray color. Black develops and darkens a lot as it sits out!*
· **Gray** *Use the residual black in the bowl to make a light gray color or add small drops of black.*
· **Brown/chocolate brown**
· **Forest green**
· **Light succulent/avocado**

Now you have a starting base for every color of the rainbow! For the fall season or just a more vintage and rustic vibe, try adding a little ivory food coloring to every color. At the bakery, we then call that color "dusty." Dusty pink, dusty blue, dusty purple, they are all so pretty and classy!

The tone of your colors should match the vibe of your cookies: I love using the forest green and light succulent as leaves on flowers for a fancier occasion. Dark green and lime green are great for leaves when the cookies are more whimsical or for spring.

For color inspiration, one of my all-time favorite things to do is to go to the paint aisle at the home improvement store. Pick out a bunch of swatches and bring them home, then color-match your icing to the swatches!

How to Make Unicorn Poo/ Rainbow Swirly Icing!

SUPPLIES
Plastic wrap
Detail icing
Spatula

This is one of the funnest techniques . . . and you will want to use this icing on *everything*. You can switch up any colors for this technique: Try red and greens for Christmas. Use pastel colors for a lighter look. The sky is the limit!

Start by laying out your plastic wrap square, just as you would before you fill a regular pod of detail icing.

Mix a little dark pink detail icing. Using a spatula, plop and spread the dark pink icing in a diagonal line on the plastic wrap.

Repeat this using light pink icing, but lay the light pink icing next to the dark pink. Make sure they touch. **See A.**

Do this again with a yellow icing, but place this directly on top of the light pink. You can smear the icings together a little bit.

Do this one more time with a turquoise icing. Place this on top of the dark pink, next to the yellow. **See B.**

Roll the pod up, diagonally corner to corner. Make sure none of the colors get wrapped away and hidden. You need to see every color from the outside of the roll or it will not show when you pipe it from the bag. **See C, D.**

Load the icing pod into the bag as you normally would, cutting the excess plastic wrap out of the end. I recommend using a tip 8 or larger when piping with this icing, so the colors don't get squeezed together too much and create a muddy look. **See E.**

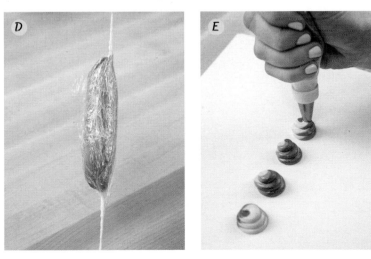

Glaze Icing

Are you ready for the easiest recipe of all time? This is the icing you will use to flood the majority of your cookie, aka the good-tasting stuff! It is sweet. It dries hard enough to ship and touch without it messing up. The bite is soft and not crunchy. It is so simple, and it requires no guesswork on consistency. Just follow this recipe exactly, and it will turn out right *every* time. This glaze icing is thin and pourable. It's not for any details that need to hold their shape, but it is perfect for covering a large surface area.

Add the powdered sugar, corn syrup, milk, and food coloring (if using) to your stand mixer. Mix until smooth, scraping the sides of the bowl once or twice. The more you mix it, the shinier it gets!

I like to mix it on medium speed until it is smooth and incorporated. Then, I turn the mixer down to the lowest speed and mix for about 5 minutes to get a lot of the air bubbles out. I have found that the longer I mix it on low speed, the shinier the icing dries. I don't know why, I just know that after making over 100,000 batches of this stuff, that is the facts.

Recipe Alterations
Substitute lemon juice for milk for a tart lemon glaze. Use orange juice for a sweet orange glaze. We have even added ¼ cup (26 g) of powdered peanut butter to the milk for a peanut butter glaze icing!

It is fine to use an extract in the glaze. Just note that it is easy to overdo it, so start with 1 teaspoon. A teaspoon of almond extract is so tasty if you are an almond fan like me!

4 lb. (1.8 kg) powdered sugar, sifted

1 cup (235 ml) light corn syrup

1¼ cups (295 ml) milk (or water or juice, see Recipe Alterations, left)

1 tablespoon (15 ml) white food coloring (optional)

Yield: Makes about 7 cups (875 g), enough for flooding three 20-cookie batches.

Coloring Glaze

Glaze icing takes *much less* colorant than royal icing to achieve a deep color. I always add white food coloring to my big batch of glaze while it is in the stand mixer. This will make the colors you mix after that turn out more opaque. If you don't have or don't want to use white food coloring, your color will just appear more translucent and slightly less vivid.

If you are making a large batch of cookies with the same color background/flood icing, dye the entire batch while in the mixer. If your cookies require different background colors, simply mix the colors in small bowls, just as you did the royal icing (page 26).

Transfer the glaze into your flood bottles by pouring a thin stream. Go slowly to avoid spilling everywhere! I do not recommend using glaze in piping bags. Even if you use the elastic bag tie, the glaze will spill out of both ends while you are not using it, and it is a complete mess. The plastic bottles on our website are definitely the way to go. Plus, when you are done, if there is any left, you can simply pop the bottles into the refrigerator and use them again next time!

Storing Glaze

Store the glaze in an airtight container in the refrigerator. If it has been in the refrigerator for a while, let the icing come to room temperature for about 1 hour before using.

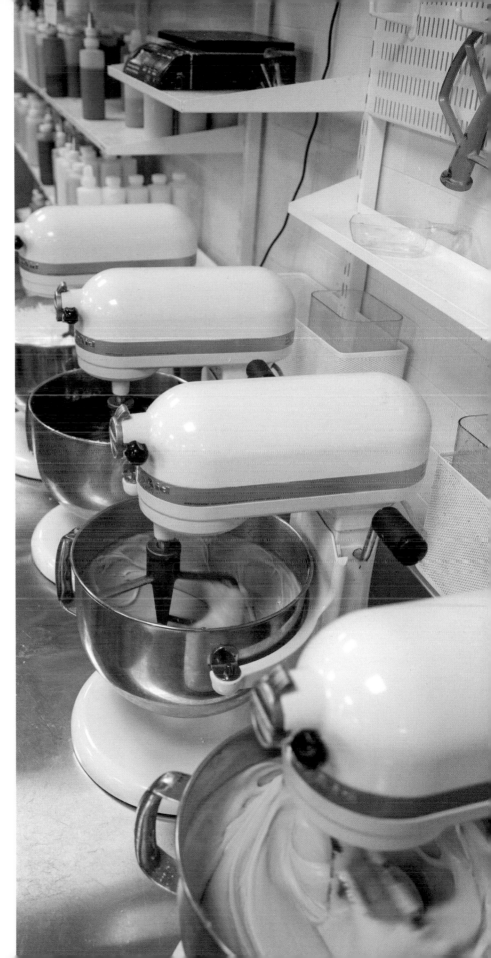

Stenciling on Cookies

Stenciling on cookies is one of the fastest ways to decorate! You can stencil nearly anything, and if you are crafty and have a Cricut cutter at home, you can even create your own stencils. You can also find countless stencil creators selling awesome designs online, or even in your local craft store. You can find some of our favorite places to buy stencils on page 185.

One of the main things to watch for when stenciling is that the detail icing you use is thick! If the icing is too thin, it will spread under the stencil and will not create crisp, clean lines when you pull the stencil away from the cookie.

You also do not want to scrape the icing thick. Once you coat the entire stencil in icing, try to scrape the excess icing off, leaving only a thin layer of icing between the stencil and the cookie. The less swipes you can do, the better. That way you don't risk the stencil moving around and messing up the lines and cookie underneath!

Don't be afraid to jazz up a stencil by piping extra details on top. Sometimes simplicity is nice if you are using the cookies as part of a set, but a stencil can look kind of flat and boring if you leave it as is. To create some dimension, add a floral border or greenery around stenciled words, or bandanas and sunglasses on top of a stenciled face!

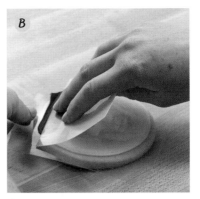

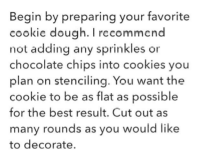

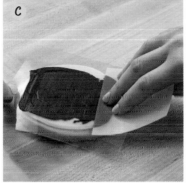

Begin by preparing your favorite cookie dough. I recommend not adding any sprinkles or chocolate chips into cookies you plan on stenciling. You want the cookie to be as flat as possible for the best result. Cut out as many rounds as you would like to decorate.

Step 1. Outline the cookie using your white detail icing. Allow the outline to set for at least 30 minutes before flooding the cookie.

Step 2. Flood the cookie with your white flood icing. Make sure that your flood icing smooths itself out completely. When stenciling on a cookie, it is crucial that you have as flat a cookie as possible. If there are any waves or dips in the icing, the stencil will not lie flat, and when you scrape icing across it, it will bleed and the design won't come out correctly.

Allow the flood icing to dry overnight. This is longer dry time than I would usually recommend, but when stenciling you are putting

pressure on the icing. If it is not dry, you will leave fingerprints and smoosh the icing!

Step 3. Place the clean, *dry* stencil on top of the dry cookie. Use one finger with gentle pressure to hold the stencil in place on the cookie. I like to hold it at the top of the cookie and scrape downwards.

Step 4. Using your black detail icing, pipe a large line of frosting onto your spatula or scraper. *See A.*

Step 5. Starting at the top of the stencil, apply the black icing and scrape downwards. You can repeat this as often as needed, but try to get it in as few swipes as possible. Always move in the

same direction when scraping. The goal is to have the stencil not move at all! *See B and C.*

Step 6. When you have a thin layer spread evenly across the stencil, slowly peel the stencil away from the cookie, leaving the design underneath! *See D.*

Voilà! The perfect cookie that almost looks *printed* on! You can leave the cookie like this or add extra details to create a little more dimension and color.

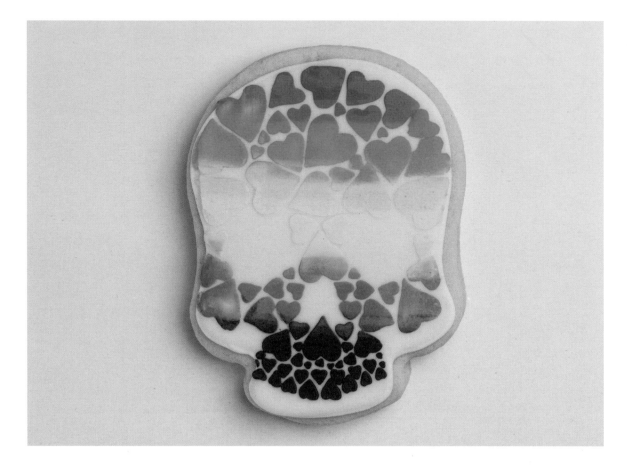

Multi-Color Option

A fun variation for stenciling on cookies is to create a rainbow or multi-color effect when smearing the icing. It is so simple and it will leave everyone wondering how in the world you got this look!

For this tutorial, I will use a skull cookie cutter and stencil.

Follow steps 1 through 3 (page 137) to get started. **See A.**

Step 4. Lay out a clean piece of plastic wrap on the table.

Step 5. Pipe thick lines of each detail icing color, touching side by side on the plastic wrap, using no tip on your piping bag. I like to go in rainbow order: red, orange, yellow, green, blue, and then purple. This will create the perfect fade from one color to the next. **See B.**

Step 6. Using your scraper, act like you are going to slice off a piece of bread, and slice about ½ inch (1 cm) of the icing, getting each color on your scraper.

Step 7. Apply the icing to the top of the stencil. Holding the stencil with a light pressure, drag the scraper downwards, covering the entire stencil and cookie. You can re-scrape the design, just keep the colors lined up.

The more times you scrape with this rainbow effect, the more of a blended look you will achieve. Make sure that when the stencil is coated you scrape any excess icing off to leave only a thin layer on top. **See C.**

Step 8. Gently peel back the stencil to reveal the COOLEST screen printed cookies you will ever see! **See D and E.**

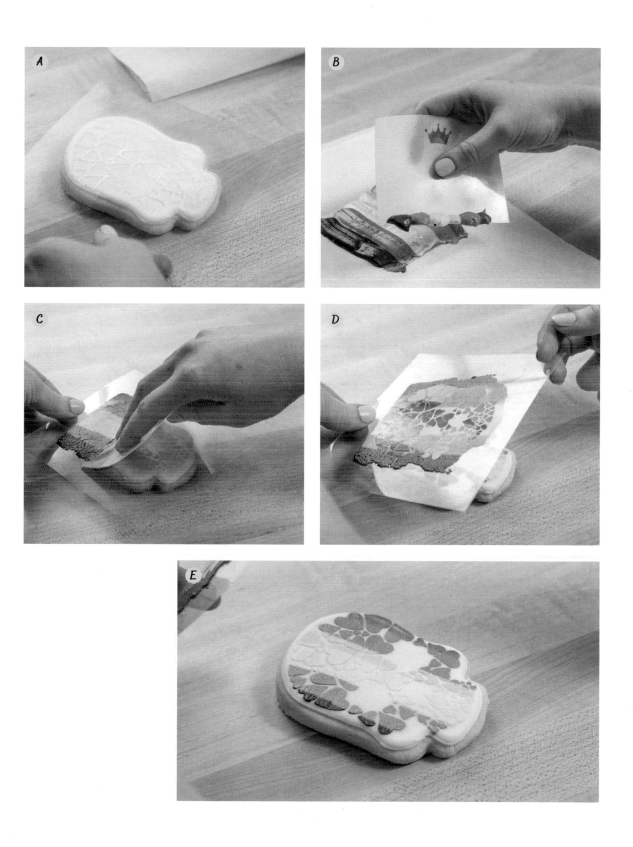

Airbrushing

Airbrushing is the quickest way to make your cookies look professional and artistic. You can add shading and gradient that you cannot get with icing alone! When airbrushing, you will need food coloring that is specific to airbrushing. Do not put regular food coloring into the airbrush or it will get all clogged up and may never work right again! You can use stencils to create pattern, or no stencil to create gradients and shading.

If You're Using Stencils

Using stencils is a quick way to get fancy or intricate designs that you may not be able to draw on the background of a cookie. It is also a cute way to make a calligraphy cookie even more detailed!

If you are using stencils, make sure your flood icing is completely dry before you airbrush, so the stencil does not stick to the icing.

I recommend getting the stencil genie to hold your stencil in place. It is a cool magnetic frame that will keep your stencil from moving while you are airbrushing. You can use a stencil by simply placing it on top of the cookie, but the air from the airbrush could blow and cause the stencil to move mid-spray. Other options are to get tiny magnets to hold the stencil in place on the corners. *See A.*

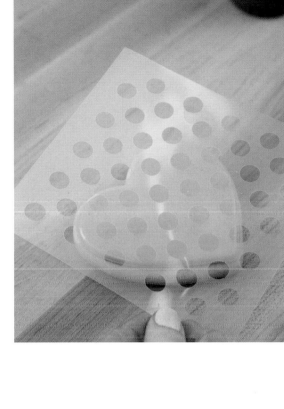

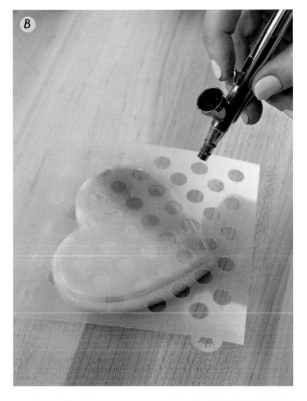

When spraying over a stencil, move the airbrush with a light spray in a slow motion back and forth in the same direction. It is better to do multiple passes of lightly sprayed color than to do one pass of heavy spray. A heavy spray could make the airbrush coloring pool up and create blotches and ruin the lines of the stencil. *See B and C.*

If You're Not Using Stencils

Creating an ombre effect is a very popular trend in everything, especially cookies! To create a single color ombre, simply load the airbrush gun with the color you want and airbrush at the top (or bottom) of your cookie. Slowly build up the color on top of itself until it is as dark as you want. Begin to slowly move down the cookie, letting up in pressure, and not making as many passes over the same place, so the color fades. **See A.**

To blend two colors, start the next color at the opposite end. Leave a middle area for the two colors to overlap. **See B.**

A rainbow fade is actually easier to make than you think! You can achieve a rainbow effect by using only three colors: red (or pink), yellow, and blue (or turquoise). Envision the cookie you are working on divided into six sections. They will be red, orange, yellow, green, blue, and purple. At either end of the cookie, in the first and sixth section, airbrush red. **See C.**

Very lightly spray the red in the second section. Rinse out your airbrush and then go back in with yellow, spraying over the red in the second section (to create orange), then spray solid yellow in space 3 and lightly spray yellow in space 4. **See D.**

Rinse out your airbrush and fill it with blue. Spray the blue lightly over the yellow in space 4, creating green. Then spray space 5 solid blue. Spray the blue lightly over the red in space 6, creating purple. **See E.**

If you want a more pastel look for your airbrush colors, add white airbrush coloring, or even a pearl sheen, before spraying. I like to mix the colors in a small ramekin or bowl before pouring them into the airbrush machine.

Whether or not you use stencils, let the airbrush coloring dry on the cookie before continuing on to top detail decoration. If you don't, the airbrush coloring may absorb into the detail icing and change the coloring.

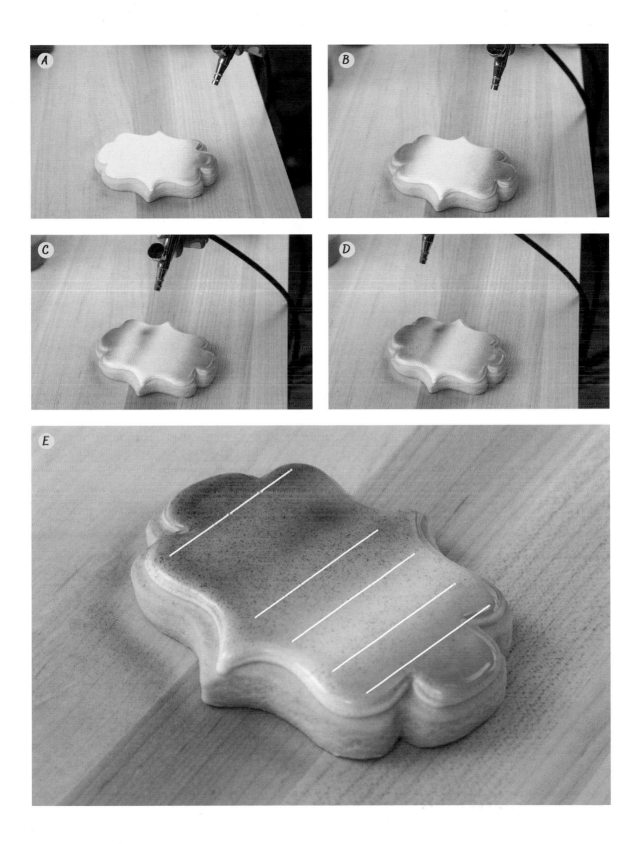

Writing Workshop

A

THIN = FLOODING

medium = flowers

writing = very thick

Now for quite possibly the *most* important part of this entire book: how to write with icing! With a lot of patience, and a little practice, you *can* do this too! Before you get started, I have a couple important notes.

ICING CONSISTENCY: MAKE IT THICK!

Don't use icing that is too thin. If your icing is too thin, after you pipe the perfect wording, it will all slowly mush together into an illegible mess. It is better to err on the side of icing that is too thick. Follow our royal icing recipe on page 22 *exactly.*

When you water it down, add just a little water at a time (about ½ teaspoon), until the icing is smooth and does not appear grainy. It should still hold a peak that curls slightly under when you lift a spatula up through the icing. *See A.*

USE THE PROPER PIPING TIPS

To get writing on your baked goods that turns out looking like a professional calligrapher did it, you *have to* use the brand specific PME 1.5 and PME 2 tips, fitted inside of a coupler and bag, as shown in our supplies section on page 12.

Practice Makes Perfect

The best way to practice is to copy the lettering templates on page 186. Tape a template down to your countertop. Then place a sheet of parchment paper on top, and tape that down. Practice by tracing these letters with your icing. Generally, I squeeze harder on the down strokes of a letter, releasing the pressure as my piping tip moves upward or to close a letter.

The harder you squeeze and slower you move, the thicker your line will be. The faster you move and softer you squeeze, the thinner your line will be.

To make sure you don't have a pointy tip at the end of a line or letter, you can stop squeezing while your piping tip is still in the icing, then slightly move the tip backward, retracing the letter. This will smooth that end off.

If your icing breaks when trying to make a smooth line, continue your letter until it is finished. Then go back to correct the hole. You can use a toothpick to smooth out any rough spots in the line. *See B.*

Getting Creative

MIXING STRAIGHT AND CURSIVE FONTS

To make a cookie look more interesting, I use a mix of straight, printed lettering, and scripty, cursive font. I usually make the words I want to be more noticeable in a cursive font. For example, the way we write "Hello" in print and "Gorgeous" in cursive. **See A.**

EXPERIMENTING WITH NEW WRITING AND FONTS

Print out your favorite font from a Word document. Tape it down to your countertop, and practice just as you did with our practice sheet in this book!

PROJECTING

One of my favorite pieces of equipment is the pico projector. This is a small projector you can clamp onto your table, plug into your phone or tablet, and project any image or writing down onto your cookie, cake, or dessert! Then you can just trace directly onto the cookie. This is definitely a bit of an investment, and obviously takes more time to use than learning to freehand directly on the cookie. Plus, it can actually limit your creativity. I encourage people to learn their own way of writing on cookies once they get the hang of it.

ICING LETTER TRANSFERS

If you don't want to write directly on a cookie, you can use the royal icing transfer technique. This means you will pipe the icing on your parchment paper,

tracing the lettering you printed out underneath. Allow the icing letter to dry for 24 hours or so. Then peel the icing off of the parchment paper and stick it onto wet icing on your cookie. If your cookie icing is dry, you can pipe a small dot of icing onto the back of the letter and "glue" it down to the cookie.

This technique can result in perfect letters, but it requires you to be very gentle. It usually results in more broken letters than perfect ones, because the royal icing is fragile. So again, the more you can practice, the better, because the most tried and true way is to pipe directly onto the cookie.

FOOD PEN

For super small writing or for drawing small facial features such as eyelashes, a food pen is

the way to go! They come in all colors and many kinds of tips. If you are writing and want to be very fastidious, I recommend the FooDoodler because the tip of the pen is harder and pointier, resulting in a smaller line. The felt-tip food pens (AmeriColor Gourmet Writer) are great for a wider line. When using a food pen, you must use a very light pressure so you don't make a hole in the cookie, and your icing needs to be completely dry.

Embellishments for Cookies with Writing

Sometimes just writing on a cookie can make a bold statement, but other times it can look plain. If you are looking for a few extra details to put on your calligraphy cookies, here are my favorite decorations!

HOW TO PIPE WIGGLE FLOWERS

Even a single flower can add a delicate detail. You can do this by piping our standard wiggle flowers, or try using a star tip to create a textured floral accent. We usually group our wiggle flowers in sets of three or five, but isolating any of these flowers by itself makes a cute accent!

The first is our center wiggle flower. To create this look, start with an uneven blob of frosting. Yes, seriously, it can be as abnormally shaped as you want. Go back on top of that blob, starting at the outer edge, and make a wavy line that spirals inward, ending in the middle of the blob. That's it! *See B.*

For the daisy flower, pipe six teardrop shapes, all ending in the same middle point. Then pipe a different colored dot in the center of the daisy. *See C.*

For the rose, pipe a smooth round blob. This is a lot like the first wiggle flower, however you want this one to be round. Pipe a smooth line on top of the blob of icing, starting at the edge and spiraling inward, ending in the center. *See D.*

For the leaves on these, I like to leave the tip number 2 on, pipe a dot, and while still squeezing, pull the dot outward, releasing pressure to create the spiked-leaf effect.

HOW TO PIPE A STAR TIP FLOWER

For this one, I use a tip number 820. This is a smaller star tip, but you can use larger if you want a larger flower. Squeeze with steady pressure, in a circular motion. Release when you have connected the start and end of your circle. With a leaf tip number 352, squeeze the fatter, base-end of your leaf. As you pull away from the base of the leaf and flower, release pressure and stop squeezing. This will create the point of the leaf! *See A.*

SPRINKLES

If you plan your cookie beforehand, you can create a cute and festive effect by sprinkling the base icing while it is wet and then writing on top. I like to use the "falling sprinkle" technique on cookies that will need a lot of writing, because it's hard to write on top of sprinkles because it is a rough surface. Start by making the sprinkles heavy at the top of the cookie, and then have them get lighter in density as you move down the cookie about one-quarter of the way, leaving you plenty of room to write underneath it. *See B.*

If you don't think to put sprinkles down while you are flooding and want to add sprinkles after you do the writing, simply pipe your writing, then go back with a tip 2, and pipe a drip-like shape over the writing. Fill it in with icing, and then add sprinkles! You can even dip that "drip" in sprinkles if your writing has dried.

SIMPLE SCROLLS

This is my favorite detail to add for a graduation or something that needs to be elegant—or even a masculine name-plaque. To make this design, I write on the cookie first. Then I pipe a curving line starting from the edge of the cookie that ends in a large curl toward the word or name.

Start below that line following the shape of it, but curl the end slightly less of a curlycue, the opposite direction, adding two more teardrop shapes under that curve. Repeat this on the top of the writing. *See C, D, E.*

INTRICATE FILIGREE

This may look intimidating, but it is a simple pattern that you turn and replicate all over the cookie. When you master the initial shape, you will have this down in no time!

This shape consists of seven teardrop shapes, some that have more of a curlycue at the end. Notice how the bottom of this shape is a V. To find where to place these shapes, look for the Vs in your cookie! You can see there is a little V indent between the lines of LOVE and YOU. Start by piping the two bottom teardrops, then add the two curlycue teardrops with the curly ends curving down. *See A, B.*

Pipe two smaller teardrops on top of the curlycues, and one more teardrop that points straight up and down, in the middle. Look for where else you can add the V-shape! When you carry that shape, turning its direction all different ways, you will create a masterpiece that is sure to impress. *See C.*

You can re-create this effect on any cookie shape, with any wording. Just always start with the writing and look for the V!

SMALL DRAWINGS THAT RELATE TO THE MESSAGE

For our taco cardio cookie, I love piping a small taco (page 82). If you have a quote about pizza, maybe a tiny slice of pizza piped underneath would be cute! The possibilities are endless. Just remember that the smaller it

gets, the harder it is to add more elements. Keep it simple so your design is recognizable without overdoing the details. This is where you can make a tiny taco royal icing transfer and stick it on later, essentially creating your own sprinkle! *See D.*

ADD A BORDER

Giving a cookie a complete finished look can be as easy as creating a simple line, a sprinkle border, a dotted border, or a beaded border. For a sprinkle border, pipe a smooth line around the edge, then dip the cookie in the sprinkles. For a beaded border, pipe a dot and continue squeezing, using heavy pressure and then lighter pressure, creating a beaded look along the edge.

Animals

Bear Face

This cookie cutter is one of my favorites, because there are so many cute animals you can turn it into! Let's start with what it was initially intended for, the cute little teddy bear!

Start by preparing your favorite cookie dough from the options on pages 19 to 21 and cutting out as many bear faces as you would like to decorate! These would pair well with a plaque with a name on it or a sweet saying such as "I love you BEARY much"! Bake your cookies according to the recipe instructions and let them cool.

Step 1. Outline the entire cookie in dark brown detail icing. Allow this to dry for at least 30 minutes before flooding. **See A.**

Step 2. Fill the cookie with the brown flood icing. Allow the flood to dry for at least 4 hours before moving on.

Step 3. Using a piping tip 5 or larger, pipe a large oval for the bear's snout, using ivory detail icing. You can use the tip of your piping bag to wiggle the icing and make it smooth out.

Step 4. Using the black detail icing, pipe two black dots for the eyes, a heart for the nose (on top of the ivory snout), and a little black smile below the snout, if you'd like.

Continued →

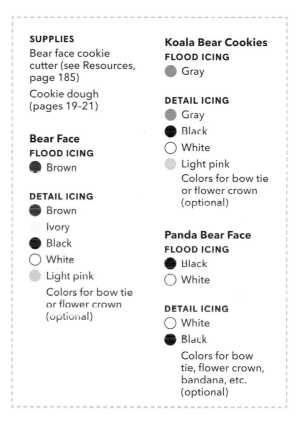

SUPPLIES
Bear face cookie cutter (see Resources, page 185)
Cookie dough (pages 19-21)

Bear Face
FLOOD ICING
● Brown

DETAIL ICING
● Brown
  Ivory
● Black
○ White
● Light pink
  Colors for bow tie or flower crown (optional)

Koala Bear Cookies
FLOOD ICING
● Gray

DETAIL ICING
● Gray
● Black
○ White
● Light pink
  Colors for bow tie or flower crown (optional)

Panda Bear Face
FLOOD ICING
● Black
○ White

DETAIL ICING
○ White
● Black
  Colors for bow tie, flower crown, bandana, etc. (optional)

A

Step 5. Always go back to the eyes and add the tiny white dots, one larger and one smaller, to make them look even cuter! **See B.**

Step 6. Add two half-circles, flat-side down, inside of the ears in your light pink detail icing and fill them in. If you feel like adding little rosy cheeks, you can do that here as well! **See C.**

From here, you can add a bow tie or an adorable flower crown! (See pages 43–44 to learn how to add floral details.) **See D.**

B

C

D

Koala Bear Cookie

Now here is a slightly different take on the same cutter!

Step 1. Outline the entire cookie around the edge in gray detail icing. Allow to dry for at least 30 minutes before flooding. *See A.*

Step 2. Fill in the entire cookie in the gray flood icing. Allow to dry for at least 4 hours or overnight before moving on. *See B.*

Step 3. Start with the nose: Pipe an oblong shape in black detail icing, with a rounded point toward the top. Still using black, pipe two dots for the eyes and a W-shape for the mouth! If you don't like the W-shape, simply pipe a smile below the nose.

Step 4. Add the white accent dots to the eyes, using your white detail icing.

Step 5. Add the light pink ears, just as we did for the teddy bear. *See C.* If you want to add your flower crown or bow tie, now is the time! We've even done a cute bandana on our koala faces before! *See D.*

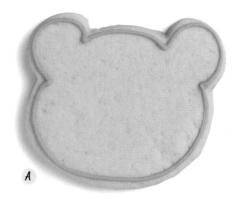

A

B

C

D

Panda Bear Face

Same cutter, different bear. So many options, so little time!

Step 1. Outline just the head shape in the white detail icing, leaving off the ears.

Step 2. Outline the ears in black detail icing. With your black icing, draw the big black eye spots that pandas are known for! These almost look like two kidney beans with the curve facing inwards. Allow the outline to set for at least 30 minutes before flooding. *See A.*

A

Step 3. Flood the black parts of the face and allow it to dry for at least 1 hour before flooding the white. This will help prevent bleeding between the two colors. If your colors do bleed together, you can usually fix it by re-outlining the eyes, head, and ears after the flood has dried. Once you have flooded both colors, let the cookie dry for at least 4 hours before moving on to top deco.

Step 4. Using your white and black detail icing, pipe two eyes inside of the bean shapes. Using the black detail icing, pipe a small heart between the eyes, for the nose, and a tiny rounded W-shape for its mouth. *See B.*

B

Step 5. Again, here you can add a single flower to the corner of its ear, a bow tie for a dapper panda, or maybe your panda will have a bedazzled head-band! *See C.*

C

Bumble BEE!

Whether you're a queen or just having a BEE day, your friends will love these cookies more than bees love honey!!

Start by preparing your favorite cookie dough from the options on pages 19 to 21 and cutting out as many bees as you would like to decorate! Bake your cookies according to the recipe instructions and let them cool.

Step 1. This entire design will be outlined in black. Start by outlining the head in a circle. Outline the body, rounding it out near the belly, and bringing it to a point at the bottom. Pipe black lines horizontally on the body to create stripes. I like to make 5 stripes so it starts and ends with a black stripe. Outline the wings. Allow the outline to dry for at least 1 hour before flooding the cookie. *See A.*

Step 2. Using yellow flood icing, flood the head and then every other stripe on the body. Flood both wings white. Allow this flood to set for at least 1 hour before moving on and flooding the remaining sections. Flood the remaining stripes on the body in black. Let the flood icing dry for at least 4 hours before moving on to top details. *See B.*

Step 3. Using your black detail icing, pipe two eyes. You can do the standard dot eyes or the swoopy eyelash eyes! Use light pink to pipe two cheeks. *See C.*

Continued →

SUPPLIES
Front-view bee cookie cutter (see Resources, page 185)
Cookie dough (pages 19–21)

FLOOD ICING
○ Yellow
○ White
● Black

DETAIL ICING
● Black
● Light pink
Colors for details (optional)

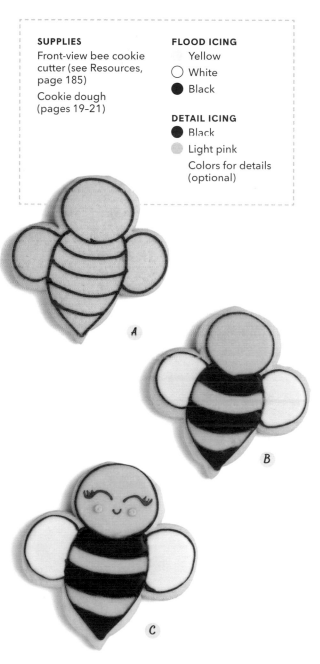

A

B

C

Step 4. Here comes your creative freedom!!! For a Valentine's Day bee, use a red detail icing to write "BEE mine" in script font across the wings and body! Or pipe two black curved lines, with two dots at the end for little bee arms and have him holding a cute heart! *See D.*

If you are celebrating a birthday, aka BEEday, splice a mini party hat cookie on top of the bee's head before baking, and decorate it like a party hat! You can finish by writing "Happy BEEday" across the bee's body!

If you're a Texan like me, or just a cowgirl at heart, splice a mini cowboy hat on top before baking and decorate using brown icing. Finish by writing "BEE-HAW!" across the bee's wings and body. *See E.*

And if you're celebrating Mother's Day, or just the queen bee in your life, splice a mini crown cookie on top of the bee's head before baking, decorate with ivory icing, and paint it gold! *See F.*

Paulette Bear

If you are wondering why we call this the paulette bear, one of the funniest problems at the bakery is naming the cutters! We had more than ten teddy bear cutters when we got this new one. And when someone asked me what to call it, the first thing that came to my mind was "paul bearer". . . ha-ha! So, we called it the paulette bear to make it a little less morbid because this bear design is ANYTHING but morbid! Literally one of the most versatile cookie shapes, this bear can transform for any season or event simply by changing what it is holding!

Start by preparing your favorite cookie dough from the options on pages 19 to 21 and cutting out as many paulette bears as you would like to decorate! If you are planning to use these as part of a set, make whatever the bear is holding into a large cookie too. For example, if it is for a girls' night out and you have the bear holding a margarita, make some large margarita shapes to put on a tray with it. Or have the bear holding a cute present and make some big birthday present shapes. Bake your cookies according to the recipe instructions and let them cool.

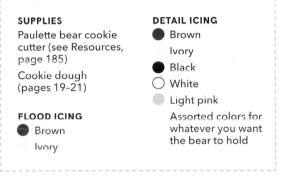

SUPPLIES
Paulette bear cookie cutter (see Resources, page 185)
Cookie dough (pages 19–21)

FLOOD ICING
● Brown
  Ivory

DETAIL ICING
● Brown
  Ivory
● Black
○ White
● Light pink
Assorted colors for whatever you want the bear to hold

Step 1. Start by outlining the entire shape in brown, including the cute little ears. You could even outline this guy white for a cute polar bear!

Step 2. Using your brown detail icing, pipe two arms. Do this by drawing two long U-shapes that slant diagonally down and in, leaving a gap big enough to pipe something between! Use your ivory detail icing to draw the belly around the arms. Make sure the arms still stay "on top" of the belly. Allow the outline to dry for at least 1 hour before flooding. *See A.*

Continued →

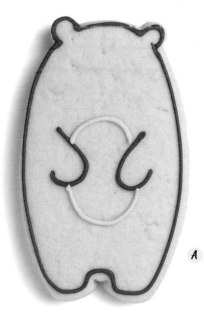

A

Step 3. Flood each section with its respective flood color, letting the brown section dry before you flood the belly so the colors will not bleed together. Allow the flood to dry for at least 4 hours before moving on to the top detail decorations. *See B.*

Step 4. Now we will draw his cute little face! Start by drawing a large oval with your ivory detail icing and filling it in with the detail icing. Pipe two small black eyes on either side of the snout, using your black detail icing. Add the small white dots to make the eyes come to life! Pipe a small black heart at the top center of the ivory snout.

I like to add two light pink dots to the sides of the snout for adorable pink cheeks! Add two half-circle details to the inside of the ears while you are still using your light pink. *See C.*

Step 5. From here the options are limitless.

Variations

For a birthday: Pipe a small rectangle between the arms. Then go back and add a cute bow to the top of the present. *See D.*

For a girls' night: Pipe a small cocktail glass by drawing a curvy glass in white, and then the stem of the glass in white detail icing. Fill that in with a dark pink icing, then add a cute yellow straw!

For Valentine's Day: Pipe a long heart or a bouquet of roses.

For something silly: Pipe a bag of potato chips! Draw a red rectangle, a yellow circle on top of the bag, and then some ivory circles coming out of the top of the bag to look like little chips!

For Halloween: Pipe paulette bear holding a cute pumpkin and make it have a cute bow tie or flower crown!

I could go on and on. . . .

B

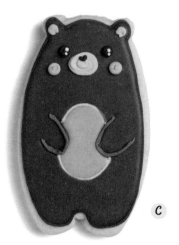

C

D

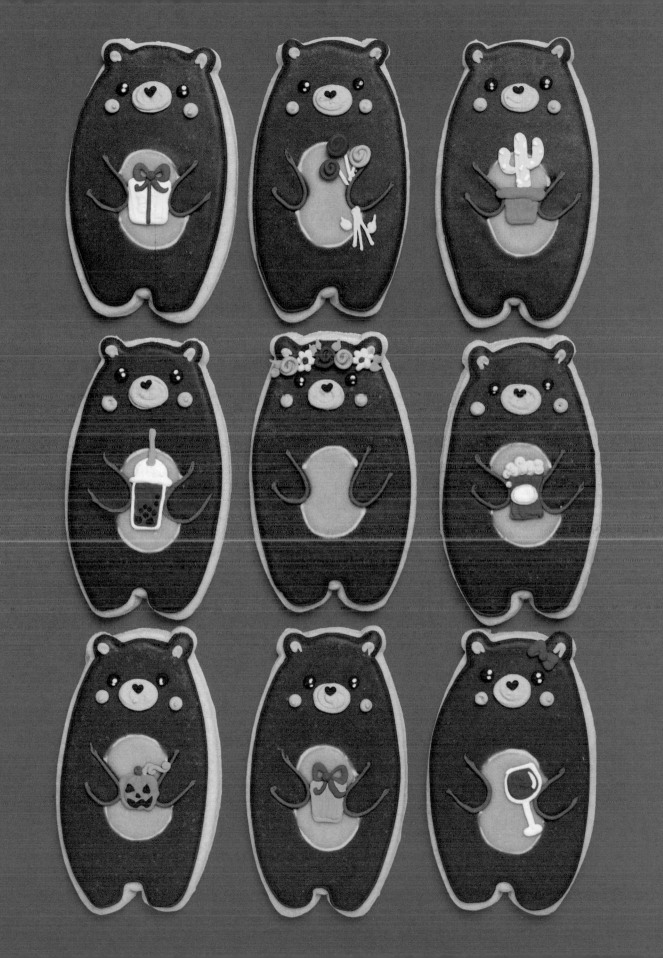

Mini Farm Animals

Okay, no matter how many cookies you cut, you will always have a few little scraps left over. One of my favorite things to cut—mostly because it's easy—is a bunch of mini rounds! You can use these for toppers on cupcakes or just as little filler details on a tray of cookies. Or just to eat while you decorate, which I highly recommend. If you are out of ideas on how to decorate them, try these cutie little farm animal faces. Bonus! Mini means you get about sixty cookies per batch!

Start by preparing your favorite cookie dough from the options on pages 19 to 21 and cutting out as many mini circles as you would like to decorate! We show you four simple farm animal faces, but these would pair well with a solid white round that you can use your airbrush to add some red plaid detailing! Bake your cookies according to the recipe instructions and let them cool.

SUPPLIES	DETAIL ICING
Round cookie cutter	Yellow
Cookie dough (pages 19–21)	● Orange
	● Black
FLOOD ICING	○ White
Yellow	● Light pink
○ White	Ivory
● Black	● Light gray
● Light pink	

Chick Face

Step 1. Outline the entire circle in yellow detail icing. Allow the outline to set for 30 minutes before flooding. Flood the circle yellow. Allow it to dry for at least 4 hours. *See A*.

Step 2. Pipe a tiny orange triangle in the center with your detail icing. Pipe two small black dots for eyes and tiny white dots for the reflection.

Step 3. Using yellow detail icing, pipe two squiggly wings on either side. I like to add a tiny tuft of yellow fluff at the top of the hair! *See B*.

A

B

Cow Face

Step 1. Outline the bottom "snout" of the cow in light pink. This is almost like a little squished football shape at the bottom of the round. Then outline the top of the cookie in white. Allow the outline to set for 30 minutes before flooding. *See A.*

Step 2. Flood the white part of the cow face: This part will be wet on wet, so be careful not to add too much flood so it doesn't overflow! Use a tip number 2 fitted on your black flood icing. Pipe irregular black spots all over the white flood for the cow's spots. I like to avoid the eye spaces, so it doesn't distract from the eyes. Next flood the light pink snout.

Step 3. When the flood has set up for at least 4 hours, pipe two small pink teardrops on top of the snout. Then pipe two black dots for eyes, smaller white dots for pupils, and two white triangles that fold over the top of the cookie for the cow's ears. Add two ivory triangles on the inner corner of the ear for the cow's little horns! *See B.*

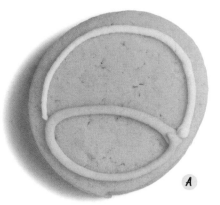

A

B

C

Sheep

Step 1. Outline the entire round in a wiggle white line, the fluffier the better for this little sheep!

Allow the outline to dry for at least 30 minutes. Flood the entire thing white with your flood icing. Allow it to set up for at least 4 hours. *See C.*

Step 2. Using light gray detail icing, pipe the head of the sheep. Start by drawing a U-shape and filling it in. Then pipe two teardrops on the top sides for the sheep's ears, still using the light gray.

Step 3. Add two small black dots for eyes and a tiny black heart at the bottom of the U for the nose. Use white detail icing to add a tiny puff of white fluff on top of the head. *See D.*

D

Pig

Step 1. Outline the round in a light pink detail icing. Allow the outline to dry for at least 30 minutes. Flood the round light pink and allow to set up for at least 4 hours before decorating on top. *See A.*

Step 2. Using light pink detail icing, pipe a large round snout and fill it in with your detail icing. Pipe two small upside-down triangles for ears at the top, flopping over the top of the head.

Step 3. Pipe two ovals on top of the snout for the cute pig nose! Pipe two black dots for eyes, with small white dots for the reflective detail. *See B.*

Note : To make some plaid filler cookies, check out our airbrushing section on page 36. Outline and flood a round cookie solid white and allow to dry. Then use a striped stencil to airbrush the stripes horizontally. Flip the stencil and airbrush on top of that vertically!

Now you're ready to start a farm! And if you're lucky, yours won't turn out as awful as the first farm animal cookies I ever made. HA! But, hey, practice makes perfect!!!

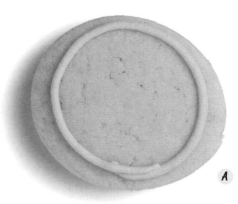

A

B

Peace-Sign Turkey

Perfect for your vegetarian Thanksgiving, these will prove you are not a regular cookie artist, you're a COOL cookie artist. These hip turkey cookies are made using a peace-sign cookie cutter. Plate them up with some "thankful, grateful, blessed" calligraphy cookies or other Thanksgiving and fall designs!

Start by preparing your favorite cookie dough from the options on pages 19 to 21 and cutting out as many peace-sign hands as you would like to decorate! Bake your cookies according to the recipe instructions and let them cool.

Step 1. Using your detail icing colors, begin by outlining the pointer finger, the thumb, and the palm all in brown. I like to start with the thumb, outlining an oblong C-shape, and wrapping that line around the bottom of the palm, ending where the pinky would start. Go back and outline the index finger.

Step 2. Using your red detail icing, outline the middle finger.

Step 3. Using orange detail icing, outline the ring finger, basically a long oval, that is behind the thumb slightly.

Step 4. Using yellow detail icing, outline the pinky finger. Allow the outline to set up for at least 30 minutes before flooding for the cleanest results. *See A.*

Step 5. Using your flood icing that matches the outline colors, fill in each color respectively. If you flood carefully and with a smaller tip, you can probably flood the colors at once, especially because we plan to re-outline each section at the end. If you are worried about the colors bleeding together, flood each color separately, allowing each color to set up for about 30 minutes to 1 hour, before flooding the next color. Allow the flood icing to dry for at least 4 hours before moving on to top details.

Continued →

SUPPLIES
Hand peace-sign cookie cutter (see Resources, page 185)
Cookie dough (pages 19–21)

FLOOD ICING
● Brown
● Orange
  Yellow
● Red

DETAIL ICING
● Brown
● Red
● Orange
  Yellow
○ White
● Black

A

Step 6. For a clean, finished look on a cookie like this, I like to go back and re-outline each section of the hand in the same color it was outlined/flooded in. This creates clean, smooth lines.

Step 7. Using your white and black detail icing, pipe an eye. To get fancy here, maybe add eyelashes for a girly turkey! **See B.**

Step 8. Using yellow detail icing, pipe the turkey's beak. I do this by piping the "less than sign" <, up right under the eye.

Step 9. Finally, using your red detail icing, pipe a long teardrop that wraps over the beak for the turkey's waddle! Betchya didn't know that thing was called a waddle! I wouldn't have known that either, but my father-in-law used to have a pet turkey, so these cookie turkeys are the only turkey I'll be able to eat for Thanksgiving! Ha-ha! **See C.**

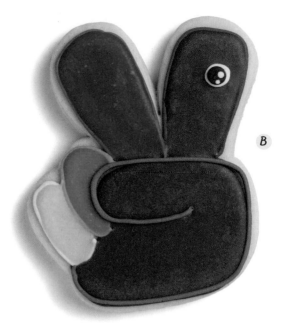

B

C

Rainbow Turtle

Okay, I feel like this little guy doesn't get enough credit. He is so happy and cute, I guarantee a smile to whoever receives these cookies! Pair these on a platter with a calligraphy cookie plaque with sayings like "Thinking of you" or "I miss the SHELL out of you!"

Start by preparing your favorite cookie dough from the options on pages 19 to 21 and cutting out as many turtles as you would like to decorate! This one would be perfect for our lemon flavor because it is bright and tart, which seems like the perfect combo for these cheery turtle cookies! Bake your cookies according to the recipe instructions and let them cool.

SUPPLIES
Turtle cookie cutter (see Resources, page 185)
Cookie dough (pages 19–21)
Brown food pen (optional)

FLOOD ICING
- Lime green
- Dark pink
- Yellow
- Turquoise

DETAIL ICING
- Dark pink
- Yellow
- Turquoise
- Lime green
- Light pink
- Orange
- Dark purple
- White
- Black
- Dark green

Step 1. Before you outline the rainbow shell, you may want to use brown food pen to lightly sketch the rough lines that will divide the shell into three arches of color. This way you have a better idea before you trace it with icing.

Step 2. I like to start with the outside of the shell. I outline the entire shell in dark pink detail icing, even the bottom. (The bottom line will get covered up later.) *See A.*

Step 3. Outline the yellow arch line and then the turquoise line.

Step 4. Using your detail lime green icing, outline the neck and head of the turtle, and his little feet, using three scallops. Allow the outline to set for at least 30 minutes before flooding the cookie. *See B.*

Continued →

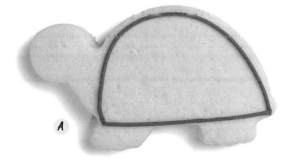

Step 5. Flood each section of the turtle with its respective color. It is not as crucial to wait between each touching color because you will be re-outlining every part of this cookie. If you have the time and are worried about the colors bleeding together too much, only flood one section at a time (the sections that do not touch each other). Allow the flood icing to dry for at least 4 hours or overnight before moving on to top deco.

Step 6. Re-outline the shell and each separate arch, using different colors. This will help create the rainbow effect. Use light pink for the top arch of the shell, orange between the yellow and pink flood, and lime green between the turquoise and yellow flood.

Step 7. Because I love the little heart detail on all my cookies, I add a small purple heart on the turquoise section of the shell, just to complete the rainbow! *See C.*

Step 8. Draw a squiggly white line to cover up the bottom line of the shell. This gives the "cloud" effect a rainbow would have!

Step 9. Pipe a cute eye, adding eyelashes if you want!

Step 10. Using lime green, add a smile and a tiny little teardrop tail coming out of the back of the shell!

Step 11. Use light pink to pipe a cute round cheek.

Step 12. Using dark green, pipe three small dots on each of the toe scallops. *See D.*

Now he is ready to go spread cheer to all of your friends! If you are pairing this with the "I miss the shell out of you" calligraphy cookies, ship these to that special pal you are missing!

Snowy Penguin

This winter guy has been playing in the snow, and he is too cute to pass up!

Start by preparing your favorite cookie dough from the options on pages 19 to 21 and cutting out as many penguins as you would like to decorate! Bake according to the recipe instructions and let cool.

Step 1. Outline the entire penguin shape in black detail icing, skipping over the feet and rounding out the bottom of the cookie.

Step 2. Using white detail icing, pipe a peanut shape inside of the black outline; but, make the top of the shape dip in like the top of a heart! Pipe two long, horizontal teardrop shapes in orange detail icing for the feet. Allow the outline to dry for at least 30 minutes before flooding. *See A.*

Step 3. Flood each section with its matching flood color. Flood the black section first and allow it to dry before flooding the white section, so the colors do not bleed together. Let the flood dry for at least 4 hours before moving on to top details. *See B.*

Step 4. With white detail icing, pipe a big, uneven line on the top of the penguin's head and dip it in a mixture of sugar crystals and rainbow nonpareil sprinkles so it looks like there's snow on his head!

Step 5. Using black detail icing, pipe two large dot eyes with the two white dots on top for reflection. Pipe a small orange triangle between the eyes and two light pink dots for cheeks.

Step 6. Using light turquoise, pipe a scarf, and fill it in with the light turquoise detail icing. Do this by piping a line across the penguin's neck, and making it a thick, curved, rectangular shape, filling it in. Pipe one rectangle that starts on the bottom edge of the right side of the scarf and goes vertically up and down, and then another rectangular shape next to that, that lies on top of the horizontal shape. *See C.*

Step 7. Add rainbow stripes with your detail icing on top of the scarf!

SUPPLIES
Penguin cookie cutter (see Resources, page 185)
Cookie dough (pages 19-21)
Sugar crystal sprinkles
Shimmery rainbow nonpareil sprinkles

FLOOD ICING
● Black
○ White

DETAIL ICING
● Black
○ White
● Orange
● Light pink
● Dark turquoise
● Dark pink
  Yellow
● Lime green
● Light turquoise
● Dark purple

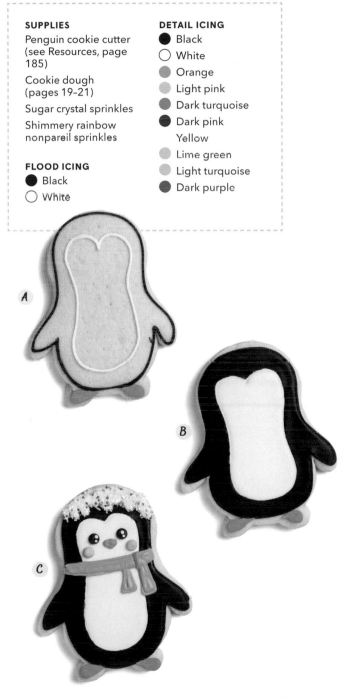

Unicorn Cookies

Okay, this shape is probably one of the most used at the bakery. Because who doesn't love a unicorn!? I will show you how to decorate this guy for three seasons, but the options are endless by changing its hair colors to match a theme or holiday! Heck, I think once we even piped a graduation hat on one!

Start by preparing your favorite cookie dough from the options on pages 19 to 21 and cutting out as many unicorn shapes as you would like to decorate! These always pair well with a rainbow (page 67). To add a calligraphy cookie, a cute plaque with the recipient's name on it or a "happy birthday" message would be perfect! Bake your cookies according to the recipe instructions and let them cool.

Step 1. Outline the body of the unicorn in white detail icing. I leave off outlining the hair because that will get covered up later with top decoration.

Step 2. Using ivory detail icing, pipe the unicorn horn. I do this by starting at the base and making tiny concentric circles that lie on top of each other and slowly get smaller as they work to the point of the horn. Allow the outline and horn to dry for at least 30 minutes before flooding.

Step 3. Flood the body white with the flood icing.

Step 4. Using your gold luster dust and clear alcohol, paint the horn gold (page 16). Allow the flood icing to dry for at least 4 hours to allow the top deco to stand out on top of the cookie. *See A.*

Step 5. Now it is time to add the facial features! I usually go with a closed squinty eye, but you can see page 51 for instructions on how to decorate faces and eyes. Then you can do an open eye if you want to! If you go with closed, use your black detail icing to pipe an upside-down U-shape, then add three flared eyelashes at the end.

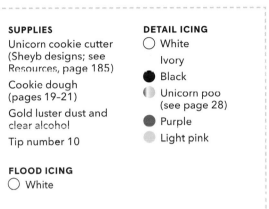

SUPPLIES
Unicorn cookie cutter (Sheyb designs; see Resources, page 185)
Cookie dough (pages 19–21)
Gold luster dust and clear alcohol
Tip number 10

FLOOD ICING
○ White

DETAIL ICING
○ White
Ivory
● Black
◐ Unicorn poo (see page 28)
● Purple
○ Light pink

A

Continued →

Step 6. With your white detail icing, retrace the unicorn's two legs closest to you (the left front and back legs). This makes it look dimensionally correct! *See B.*

Step 7. Using the white detail icing, add a small teardrop shape for the nose and add a smile!

Step 8. Pipe a round pink cheek using detail icing.

Step 9. Using the purple detail icing, I like to add a small heart near the booty! But you could add a number here for a birthday celebration, a star, or some other cute design you think up! *See C.*

Step 10. Okay, this will be the *most fun* part. For the unicorn poo (see page 28) decoration, I use the standard colors (yellow, turquoise, light pink, and dark pink). With a tip 10 fitted on the bag, I pipe a swirl that goes on top of the head, slightly over the horn, swooping upwards. Then I add the hair on the back of the neck by layering two swoops that slightly overlap each other, like a backward J-shape.

Note: The curvier you make the hair, the more it will appear to "flow" like real hair!

Step 11. Pipe the hair on the tail, again making two piping lines, one a regular sideways S-curve, and one that overlaps it from below, but swirls into a spiral at the end. *See D.*

There ya have it! The perfect rainbow unicorn!

Skele-corn

Now, let me show you how to make a spooky Halloween Skele-corn! Use the same supplies as above, but switch to gray icing on the horn and silver luster dust instead of gold! I like to add silver edible glitter as well! You also may want to switch the rainbow unicorn poo hair to Halloween colors.

Step 1. Start by outlining the unicorn in black detail icing, and using a gray for the horn. Allow to dry for at least 30 minutes before flooding.

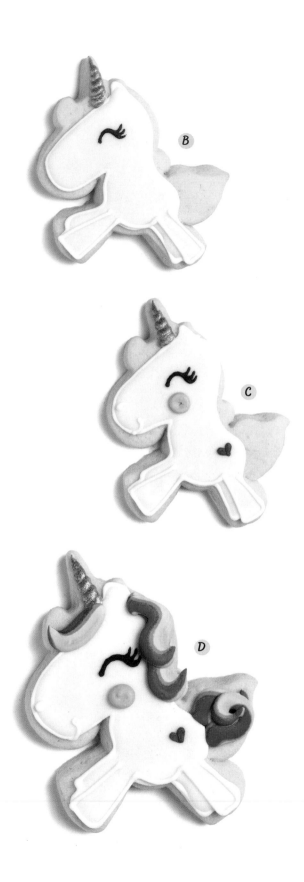

Step 2. Flood the unicorn black, and while the icing is still wet, lightly sprinkle the edible silver glitter over the icing.

Step 3. Paint the horn with your silver luster dust and clear alcohol (page 16). Once you have allowed your icing to set up for about 4 hours, you can move on to the top decoration. *See A.*

Step 4. This is where you will draw the unicorn skeleton! I like to start with the skull. Using white detail icing, following the shape of the head, just smaller, start with the ear, swoop down around the nose and round it back up to close the skull.

Step 5. Pipe a round eye socket (this will not get filled in) and a tiny dot inside of the eye. I also pipe half of a heart and a smile that won't get filled in either. *See B.*

Step 6. Fill in the skull with your white detail icing, using the end of your tip to wiggle the icing around and smooth it as best you can. If you have extra white flood icing, you can use that. If not, using the detail icing will work just fine.

Step 7. Now for the backbone and ribs! Pipe a curved line from the neck to the rear and then five or so perpendicular lines for the ribs.

Step 8. Pipe bones for the legs. I do the two legs in the foreground (just as the legs in the regular unicorn are re-outlined), piping a small heart, followed by a long line and another upside-down heart to create the perfect "bone" shape! I pipe just half of a bone for the other two legs, as if they are just peeking out behind the front legs. *See C.*

Step 9. Now for the spooky hair! You can use rainbow icing here or create a custom unicorn poo that is more fitting for Halloween—try using orange, purple, lime green, and dark green! *See D.*

Gingerbread Unicorn

Now that you are getting the hang of this cookie, it is time for the cutest unicorn of the bunch! Again, the supplies are similar but this time we want the unicorn to be brown, like a gingerbread boy, and I switch the heart to red. You also may want to switch the rainbow unicorn poo hair to Christmas colors.

Step 1. Outline and flood the cookie the same as you did in the original unicorn tutorial, but with brown.

Step 2. Retrace the legs, nose, and mouth in brown, and pipe a snoopy black eye. **See A.** I am using the same facial features as the first unicorn, with a pink cheek, but I am putting a red heart on the booty this time to match our Christmas theme!

Step 3. To make this cookie look like a gingerbread boy, use your white detail icing to add wavy white lines to the top of the head and the ends of the legs that you've outlined. **See B.**

Step 4. Using unicorn poo in Christmas colors—red, white, and green—or your regular unicorn poo, pipe the hair! **See C.**

Now, which type of unicorn are you going to make first!?

Food

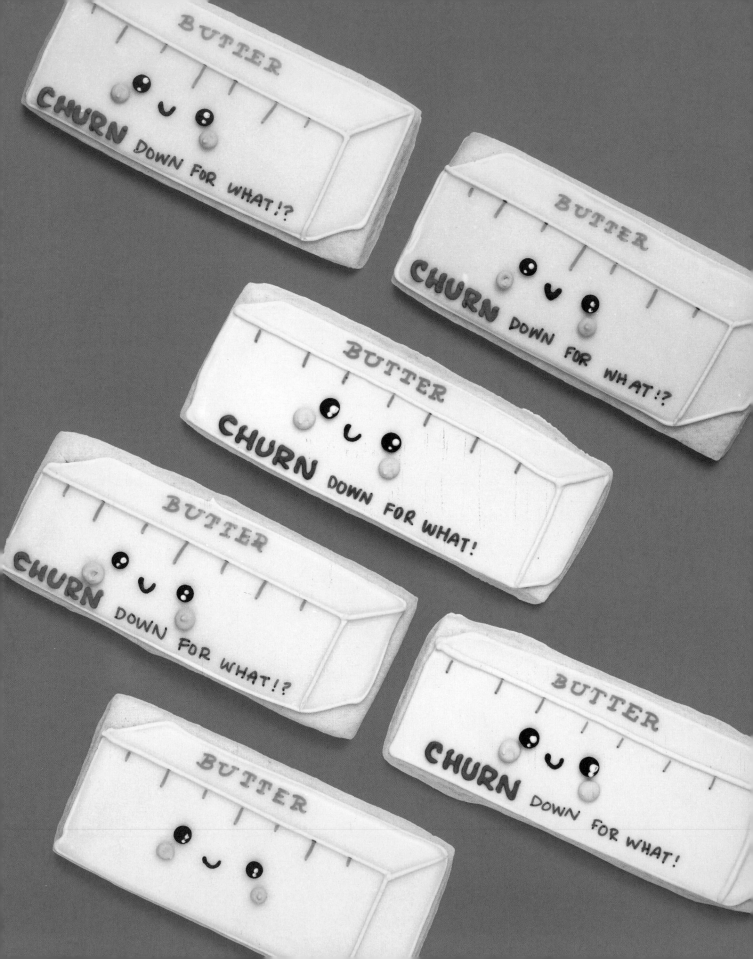

CHURN Down for What!?

If you need a hype man, look no further, these cookies are here for you. Because the cookies get writing *on* the cookie, you don't need to pair these with a calligraphy cookie—although, if you can pull off a Paula Deen face cookie, more power to ya!

Start by preparing your favorite cookie dough from the options on pages 19 to 21 and cutting out as many butter stick rectangles as you would like to decorate! Bake your cookies according to the recipe instructions and let them cool.

Step 1. Outline the rectangle with your pastel yellow detail icing, without following the shape exactly. To create the 3-D look, put a straight line across the bottom, stopping about 1 inch (2.5 cm) from the corner. Then draw a line diagonally that goes about ½ inch (1 cm) up the side of the rectangle. Outline the next corner as normal. Pipe the top edge of the cookie from right to left, ending again about 1 inch (2.5 cm) from the corner. Pipe a diagonal line, parallel to the other diagonal line, then close the outline. Whew, that was the hardest part, I promise! Allow the outline to dry for at least 30 minutes. ***See A.***

Step 2. Flood the entire shape with your pastel yellow flood. Allow the flood to dry at least 8 hours or overnight, until the icing is dry. You want the icing dry because the food pen will not work if it is wet. ***See B.***

Continued →

Continued →

SUPPLIES
Long rectangle cookie cutter (or simply cut out a rectangle with a knife!) (See Resources, page 185)
Cookie dough (pages 19–21)
Red food pen

FLOOD ICING
Pastel yellow

DETAIL ICING
Pastel yellow
● Black
○ White
● Light pink

A

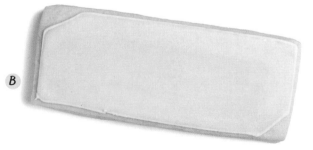

B

Step 3. Re-outline the front section of the butter stick by drawing a 3-D box, like you learned in grade school. Now you have your complete butter-stick shape! *See C.*

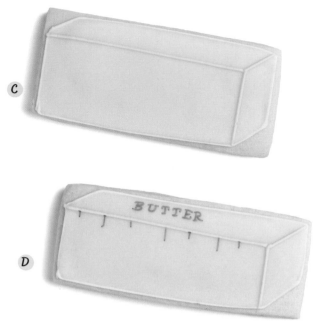

C

Step 4. Use your red food pen to draw small dash marks at the top of the butter stick, on the front view and top view, just like the tablespoon markers on a real stick of butter. Using the red food pen, write the word "BUTTER" in all caps on the top of the butter stick. *See D.*

Step 5. Pipe two black dots for eyes at the top of the front face of the butter stick, with a small U for a mouth. Add two light pink cheeks. *See E.*

D

Step 6. NOW you have a few options! If you're just having fun, try writing "CHURN down for what!" in food pen, under the face! One of my favorite Valentine's Day options is "You BUTTER be my valentine!" *See F.*

E

F

Food Truck Cookies

Okay, this food truck can be turned into basically any food you want, and that is why it is so fun!! Its initial use was an ice cream truck, but a few simple modifications to colors and details create a cute taco truck! Pair these with some writing cookies like "Feed me and tell me I'm pretty."

Start by preparing your favorite cookie dough from the options on pages 19 to 21 and cutting out as many food trucks as you would like to decorate! Bake your cookies according to the recipe instructions and let them cool.

Step 1. Outline the wheels: I like to use a larger tip (tip 10) here, so you don't have to go back and flood such a tiny space. Outline the truck in white, skipping the top part where the cone will be. **See A.**

Step 2. Use your light turquoise detail icing to pipe an L-shape for the front window and another long rectangular box where the side window will go. Allow the outline to dry for at least 1 hour before flooding, for best results.

Step 3. Using your white and light turquoise flood icing, fill in the respective colors. Allow the flood icing to dry for at least 4 hours before moving on to the top decorations!

Step 4. Use ivory detail icing to pipe the cone part of the ice cream cone on top of the truck.

Using a swirling motion and the light pink detail icing, pipe the soft serve ice cream swirl on top. While that pink is still wet, sprinkle some rainbow nonpareils on top for a fun POP of color! **See B** (next page).

Step 5. Pipe a white ledge under the long side window using white detail icing, the white half-circles above the wheels, and a white headlight. You can even add two lines to act as the "reflection" in the front window.

Continued →

SUPPLIES
Ice cream truck cookie cutter (see Resources, page 185)
Cookie dough (pages 19–21)
Ice cream cone sprinkles
Rainbow nonpareil sprinkles
Tip number 10

FLOOD ICING
○ White
● Light turquoise

DETAIL ICING
○ White
○ Ivory
● Light pink
● Black
● Light turquoise
● Dark pink
● Orange
● Yellow
● Lime green
● Dark turquoise
● Dark purple
● Red

Step 6. The details from here are up to you. My favorite thing to add on the ice cream truck is the rainbow triangle bunting! Start with a black line that will serve as your "string" for the bunting to hang from. I start about one-third of the way down from the top of the truck, and make it slope upward toward the front window. Working in rainbow order with your detail icing, pipe triangle flags hanging off the black string! *See C.*

Note: Another option is to wait until your icing is dry, then pipe a thick straight line instead of your black string. Dip that entire line in sprinkles and it will look like a fun sprinkle banner!

Step 7. For the finishing touch, I love these mini ice cream sprinkles. I pipe a tiny dot of our detail icing on the back of each one and stick them along the side of the truck. So cute!

Taco Truck

Turn this same cutter into a taco truck! Substitute the white truck for a light gray, if you want to.

Step 1. Outline and flood in the same way, but instead of piping the ice cream cone on top, start with your ivory detail icing and pipe a half-circle and fill it in for the taco shell. I use tiny black sugar sprinkles to make the taco-effect look more realistic!

Step 2. Use your green detail icing to pipe some lettuce and brown detail icing for meat. Add a perfect white dollop of sour cream on top using your white detail icing.

Step 3. Now it's coming together! Pipe the word "TACOS" on the side or bust out your food pen and write "Tacos are my love language." You can stick with the same triangle bunting or even a dotted string-light detail. Start with the same black line, then pipe small dots instead of triangles. *See D.*

Egg & Bacon

We go together like . . . Duh. Eggs and bacon! The perfect breakfast combo! How fun would these be to give your brunch-loving bestie for galentine's day!? This would be so cute to pair with a fancy plaque with writing like "Brunch buddies!" or the classic saying: "We go together like . . . "

Start by preparing your favorite cookie dough from the options on pages 19 to 21 and cutting out as many eggs-and-bacon cookies as you would like to decorate! Bake your cookies according to the recipe instructions and let them cool.

Step 1. Outline the wavy edge of the egg in white detail icing. Yeah, it will be an over easy egg, because that is the RIGHT WAY to eat eggs. Ha-ha!!

Step 2. Pipe a circle in yellow inside of the white egg shape. This will be the yolk! Remember: you don't want your yolk to be too small if you want to add a face to this at the end.

Step 3. Outline the bacon in red, using a wavy line. The bacon will be slightly behind the egg shape. Allow the outline to set up at least 30 minutes before flooding, for the best results. *See A.*

Step 4. Flood the yolk with the yellow flood icing.

Step 5. This will be wet on wet, so remember to work quickly! Flood the bacon in red flood icing. While the icing is wet, use your white detail icing and pipe wavy lines, like the fat in bacon! Do this wet on wet so it lies flat and a face can be smoothly piped on top! Let this set 1 hour before flooding the white of the egg.

Step 6. Flood the white of the egg using white flood icing. *See B.*

Step 7. Add a face to the yellow yolk using black and light pink detail icing. (See our how to draw faces section on page 51.) *See C.*

SUPPLIES
Egg and bacon cookie cutter (see Resources, page 185)
Cookie dough (pages 19–21)

FLOOD ICING
○ Yellow
● Red
○ White

DETAIL ICING
○ White
● Red
● Black
  Yellow
● Light pink

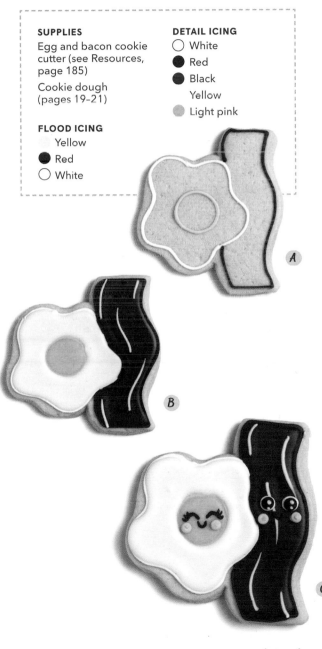

Girl, You're a FINE-apple!

Get yourself in a tropical state of mind with these sweet-and-sassy pineapple cookies! You will use your wet-on-wet technique to make these cookies next-level awesome!

Start by preparing your favorite cookie dough from the options on pages 19 to 21 and cutting out as many pineapples as you would like to decorate! Bake your cookies according to the recipe instructions and let them cool.

Step 1. Use your yellow detail icing to outline the bottom portion of the pineapple, skipping over the leaves. Take your lime green detail icing and outline the top leaves of the pineapple, bringing each to a point at the top. Allow the outline to dry for at least 30 minutes before flooding. *See A.*

Step 2. This step is wet on wet, so work quickly and don't put too much yellow flood down at first, to prevent overflow! Fill the pineapple with yellow flood, then pipe parallel lines with white *detail* icing, diagonally across the pineapple. Then reverse the lines and intersect them diagonally the other direction! *See B.*

Step 3. Flood the top leaves of the pineapple with lime green flood icing. Allow the flood to dry for at least 8 hours before moving on to top details.

Continued →

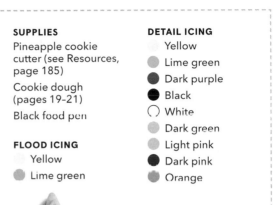

SUPPLIES
Pineapple cookie cutter (see Resources, page 185)
Cookie dough (pages 19-21)
Black food pen

FLOOD ICING
Yellow
Lime green

DETAIL ICING
Yellow
Lime green
Dark purple
Black
White
Dark green
Light pink
Dark pink
Orange

Step 4. Use dark purple detail icing to pipe two hearts, connected by a line in the middle for the sunglasses, near the top of the pineapple. Fill in the hearts with black detail icing. Add a white swipe of icing to create the reflective look.

Step 5. Re-outline the top leaves in a dark green detail icing. Using light pink detail icing, pipe cute lips under the sunglasses. I do this by drawing a wide M-shape, and then a wide U-shape under-neath that!

Optional: Use both pinks and orange detail icing to pipe three wiggle flowers at the top of the pineap-ple head, where the leaves start. (See page 43 for how to pipe wiggle flowers.)

Note : The next step requires a food pen, so make sure the cookie is super dry before trying to write!

Step 6. Now you have the perfectly sweet pineap-ple! If you're feeling sassy, use your dark pink detail icing to pipe "GIRL" in a scripty, cute font. Use your black food pen to write "you're a" underneath that. Use light pink detail icing to write "FINE-APPLE" below the food pen. *See C.*

C

✱* This is a new wet-on-wet version, as you will actually use white detail icing for the lines, while the flood is still wet. The detail icing creates a straighter, cleaner line. For any wet-on-wet stripe, I always use a base flood icing, and do the stripes in royal icing while it is still wet, so they sink into the flood.

Lemons & Footballs

Oh, you think the two don't go together? Well, you haven't visited cookie-land, where the same cutter can be used for both! Let's squeeze the day and start with this sour lemon!!

Start by preparing your favorite cookie dough from the options on pages 19 to 21 and cutting out as many football shapes as you would like to decorate! I always make the lemon dough and lemon flood icing when I am making these lemon cookies. It is the perfect addition to these cookies when they taste as good as they look! Bake your cookies according to the recipe instructions and let them cool.

Step 1. Outline the entire cookie in yellow detail icing. I like to make the ends slightly pointier when outlining it for a lemon. *See A.* Allow outline to dry for at least 30 minutes before flooding. Flood the entire cookie yellow. Allow the flood to set for at least 4 hours before moving on to top detail. *See B.*

Step 2. If you have an airbrush and want to take these cookies up a level, use orange airbrush color to add an accent of orange on top of the lemon. Use a very light hand to spray.

Step 3. Use your detail icing to pipe two black swoop eyes with eyelashes and a cute U mouth between. Pipe two light pink cheeks.

Step 4. Leave the lemon as is or add the "squeeze the day" writing at the bottom. *See C.*

Step 5. If you prefer, you can pipe "Squeeze" in dark pink script font: try practicing a few times by placing parchment paper over the cookie below, before you pipe it directly on the cookie!

Use your black food pen to write "the day" in a straight, print font.

Continued →

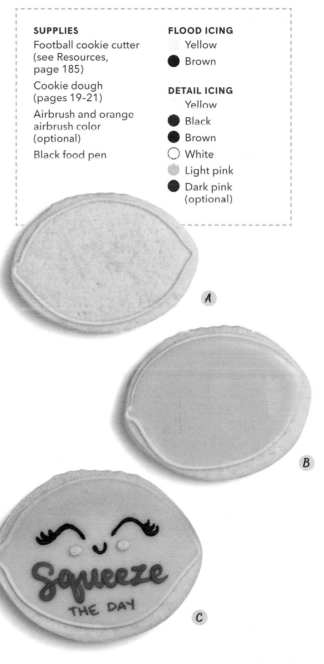

SUPPLIES
Football cookie cutter (see Resources, page 185)
Cookie dough (pages 19-21)
Airbrush and orange airbrush color (optional)
Black food pen

FLOOD ICING
○ Yellow
● Brown

DETAIL ICING
Yellow
● Black
● Brown
○ White
Light pink
● Dark pink (optional)

Variation: Now, let's play ball! Wrong sport, but still, here's some footballs! (A chocolate cookie here would be killer good!) Outline the same shape in a dark brown detail icing. *See D.* Flood the entire cookie with brown glaze icing. *See E.* Allow the flood to dry for at least 4 hours before moving on to the details. Use white detail icing to pipe two thick stripes that curve outward on both ends of the ball. Pipe a straight line down the center of the football, with small lines lying over your initial line. *See F.* TOUCHDOWN!

D

E

F

Pie til I Die

If you haven't eaten four kinds of pie until you can hardly breathe, is it really even Thanksgiving? These cookies will give you an extra pie to serve at your family feast. Make a perfect pair with a "Pie til I Die" calligraphy cookie on a fancy plaque shape!

Start by preparing your favorite cookie dough from the options on pages 19 to 21 and cutting out as many pie shapes as you would like to decorate! Bake your cookies according to the recipe instructions and let them cool.

Step 1. Use your red detail icing to start on a cherry pie! Squirt some red icing on the pie top. Use a spatula or knife to smear it in a thin layer across the top section of the pie. *See A.*

Step 2. Use ivory detail icing to pipe a dome for the pie top and a line underneath to complete the half-circle. Pipe three small hearts for "holes" on top of the crust! You will not be filling inside the hearts, so make sure any extra icing does not end up inside the hearts. If you are not feeling the heart shapes, simply pipe teardrop shapes for a more traditional pie! *See B.*

Continued →

SUPPLIES
Pie cookie cutter (see Resources, page 185)
Cookie dough (pages 19–21)
Black food coloring
Paintbrush
Water or clear alcohol

FLOOD ICING
● Dusty blue
○ Ivory

DETAIL ICING
● Red
○ Ivory
● Dusty blue
○ White

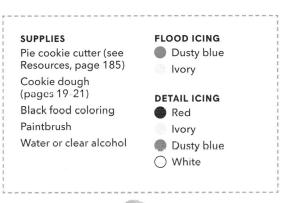

A

B

Step 3. Use dusty blue detail icing to pipe the pie plate underneath the pie top. Allow the outline to dry for at least 30 minutes before moving on to flooding.

Step 4. Start by flooding the bottom pie plate with dusty blue. Before flooding any other section, put your black food coloring in a small paint palette or dish. Add a few drops of water/alcohol and fill your paintbrush. Gently tap on the paintbrush while hovering over the pie plate, creating a splatter effect on top of the plate. Try to be careful here and not get the black all over the red on the top of the pie! *See C.*

Step 5. Use ivory flood icing to flood the top section of the pie, but NOT inside of the hearts. Allow the flood icing to dry for at least 4 hours before moving on to top detail decorations. *See D.*

Step 6. Use ivory detail icing to pipe a squiggly line where the pipe plate and the crust meet. This may be the only time I ever make a perfect pie crust! If your teardrop or heart shapes don't look as clean as you would like here, you can re-outline them with ivory detail icing to make them a little more crisp!

Step 7. Use white detail icing to pipe a cute dollop of whipped cream on top, and you are all done! Try experimenting with different colors for the pie plates, polka-dotted pie plates, or even solid colors to make a cute assortment!

Whimsy Coffee Mug

This coffee mug is the perfect cookie to make when you just want something cheery and fun! Add a finishing snowflake or wording detail to fit it to any occasion! I love pairing these with snowflake cookies in the winter or some simple name plaques for your BFF who loves to meet you for a coffee date.

Start by preparing your favorite cookie dough from the options on pages 19 to 21 and cutting out as many coffee mugs as you would like to decorate! Bake your cookies according to the recipe instructions and let them cool.

Step 1. Use your light turquoise detail icing to trace the outside of the cup. Make the line at the top (under the whipped cream) dip slightly down, like the curve of a cup. Bypass the handle of the mug for the first outlined section.

Step 2. Outline the handle of the mug: You can make it super thin or thicker, depending on what you think looks best.

Step 3. Outline the whipped cream with your white detail icing. This cutter has a designated space for cinnamon sticks! You can add brown cinnamon sticks here or you can pipe the cutest little candy cane like we will do! Use your white detail icing to pipe a hooked candy cane shape. You don't want to flood such a tiny space, so fill the candy cane in with your royal icing or use a larger tip (like a number 10) to make that line thick. Allow the outline the dry for at least 1 hour before flooding. *See A.*

Continued →

Continued →

SUPPLIES
Coffee cup with whipped cream cookie cutter (see Resources, page 185)
Cookie dough (pages 19-21)
Sprinkles
Number 10 tip (optional)

FLOOD ICING
○ White
● Light turquoise

DETAIL ICING
● Light turquoise
○ White
● Brown
● Dark pink
● Light pink
● Orange
  Yellow
● Lime green
● Dark turquoise
● Dark purple

A

Step 4. The top whipped cream will get sprinkles, and I like to flood that part first in white so the sprinkles cannot get stuck on the mug! I'm using a mix of sugar crystals and shimmery rainbow nonpareils.

Step 5. Flood the turquoise cup and handle. Allow the flood to dry for at least 4 hours before adding top detail decorations. *See B.*

Step 6. Use your light turquoise detail icing to pipe a line at the top of the cup to make a clean break between the mug and the whipped cream.

Step 7. Working in rainbow order, add the stripes to the candy cane! After that, my favorite thing to do is write the word "COCOA" in tall, skinny, rainbow letters on the cup. Mixing up a few snowflakes on the cup or adding your best friend's name is the perfect detail, too! *See C.*

Note: To turn this cup into a valentine's mug, change the candy cane into a glittery heart and flood the cup a pretty shade of light pink. Write "XOXO" or draw a cute heart.

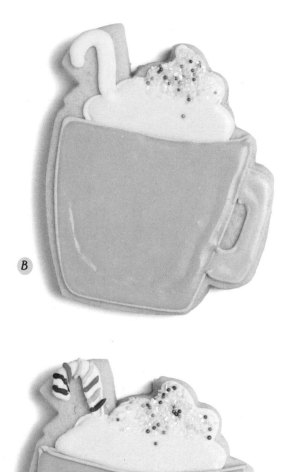

B

C

Christmas

Tree-Rex Cookies!

If you have a dinosaur-lover in your house, or you are just tired of the standard Christmas cookies, these Tree-rex cookies have your back! I like to use a standard T-Rex cookie cutter you can find almost anywhere and splice a star on top of his head. You could also use this splicing method to add a grad cap or a party hat for a birthday. These would be great to pair with some "Merry Christmas" cookies or even more traditional Christmas cookies.

Start by preparing your favorite cookie dough from the options on pages 19 to 21 and cutting out as many T-Rex cookies as you would like to decorate! (Note that our T-Rex cutter does not include the star shape on top of his head. That part needs to be added by hand.) Bake your cookies according to the recipe instructions and let them cool.

Step 1. Outline the T-Rex using the lime green detail icing. Leave off the star and create the rounded shape of the T-Rex head.

Step 2. Use yellow detail icing to pipe the yellow star that will serve as the "tree topper" on top of the T-Rex's head. Fill it in a solid yellow. Pipe a small line connecting the bottom of the star to the top of the T-Rex head. Allow the outline to set for at least 30 minutes before flooding. *See A.*

Continued →

SUPPLIES
T-Rex cookie cutter
(see Resources,
page 185)

Mini star cookie
cutter (see Resources,
page 185)

Cookie dough
(pages 19–21)

Christmas sprinkles

FLOOD ICING
● Lime green

DETAIL ICING
● Lime green
  Yellow
○ White
● Black
● Dark green
● Red

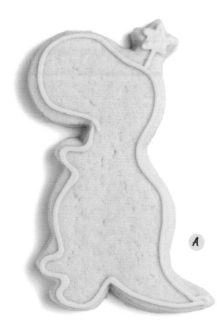

A

Step 3. This step will be wet on wet, so don't flood too many at once! Flood the T-Rex body using the lime green flood icing. While the icing is still wet, sprinkle your Christmas sprinkles on the back of the body, spreading them down into the back of the tail. Allow the flood icing to dry for at least 4 hours before moving on. *See B.*

Step 4. Using lime green detail icing, re-outline the arm and leg of the T-Rex. Add a teardrop for the nose and a small smile.

Step 5. Pipe an eyeball! You can use our basic black and white eyeball, or keep it simple and do just a black dot. (See page 51 for how to pipe facial details.)

Step 6. If you like your T-Rex as is, then leave it! I like to add a few string lights to make it look like the T-Rex got all caught up decorating himself as the Christmas tree! To do this, pipe two black lines, one sloping up, and one sloping down, as if they are wrapping around his belly and back. Add round little Christmas lights in dark green, white, and red. Now you have the perfect silly little dinosaur! *See C.* Try changing the string-light colors, sprinkles, and star to create a "birthday party T-Rex!"

B

C

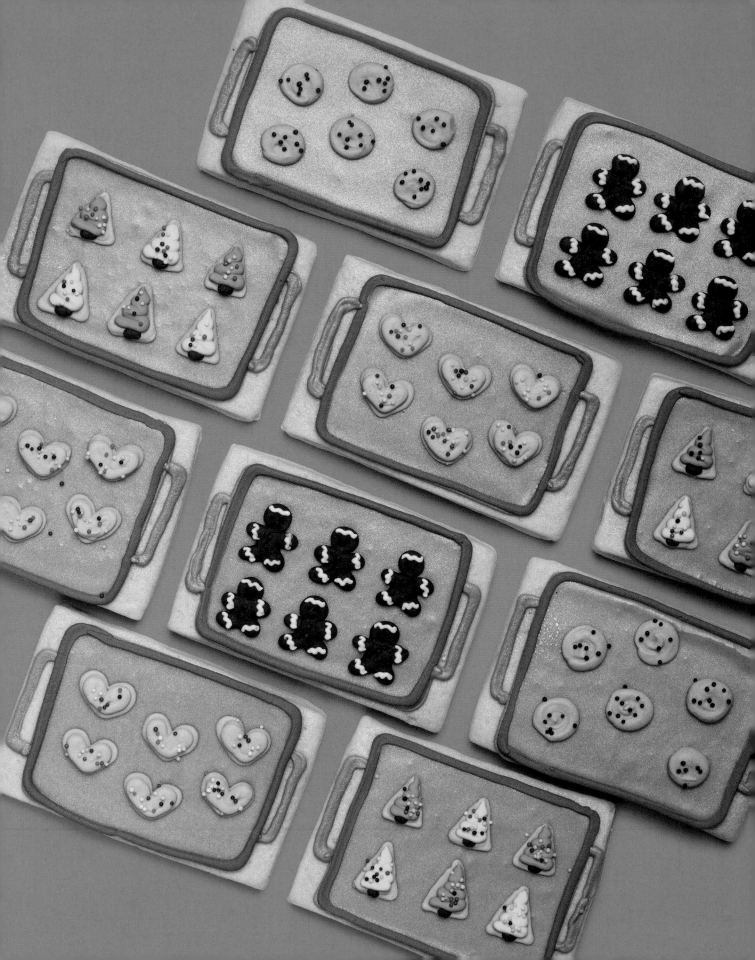

Christmas Cookie Tray

This may be one of our bakery's most popular Christmas cookie designs! I think because it's just so meta! Little cookies of LITTLE COOKIES! Who doesn't love something that cute!

Start by preparing your favorite cookie dough from the options on pages 19 to 21 and cutting out as many rectangles as you would like to decorate! You can pair these with some larger versions of the cookies you pipe on the tray, such as large Christmas trees, gingerbread boys, or even some calligraphy cookies to get you in the holiday spirit like "baking spirits bright!" Bake your cookies according to the recipe instructions and let them cool.

Step 1. Outline the rectangle in light gray, leaving about ½ inch (1 cm) on both sides of the tray.

Step 2. Pipe two gray handles, like little brackets [ ] on either side of the tray. Allow the outline to dry for at least 30 minutes. *See A.*

Continued →

SUPPLIES

Rectangle cookie cutter (see Resources, page 185)

Cookie dough (pages 19-21)

Silver airbrush color and airbrush or silver luster dust and clear alcohol

PME 1.5 tips (optional; for small details)

FLOOD ICING

- Light gray

DETAIL ICING

- Light gray
- Colors for details (optional)

Tree Cookies
- Ivory
- Lime green
- Dark green

Chocolate Chip Cookies
- Ivory
- Dark brown or black nonpareil sprinkles

Gingerbread Boy Cookies
- Brown
- White
- Red

Heart Cookies
- Ivory
- Light pink
- Rainbow nonpareil sprinkles

A

Step 3. Flood the inside of the tray with your light gray flood icing. Allow the flood to dry for at least 4 hours or overnight. *See B.*

Step 4. Re-outline the main square of the cookie sheet with light gray, making the line thicker than usual. This will create some dimension as the edge of a cookie sheet would have a little lip. *See C.*

Step 5. Airbrush a light silver sheen over the entire cookie sheet to create the metallic effect. Or use your silver luster dust and clear alcohol to paint the silver on (page 16). (You can also leave the cookie tray gray.)

Step 6. Design your cookies for your cookie sheet! *See D.*

Variations

For Christmas trees: Use ivory detail icing to pipe a basic triangle tree shape, coloring it in. I usually can fit about six cookies on the tray. Pipe a little brown base of the tree on top of the ivory. Make it small enough to still see the ivory "cookie" underneath. Using lime green or dark green, pipe a zigzag line that starts wide at the base of the "cookie" shape and goes into a point at the top. While that icing is still wet, sprinkle your rainbow nonpareil sprinkles on top. *See E.*

For little chocolate chip cookies: Use ivory detail icing to pipe large round shapes on top of the cookie sheet. *See F.* While the icing is still wet, use your black or brown nonpareil sprinkles to create little chocolate chips on top of the cookies! *See G.*

For gingerbread boy cookies: Use brown detail icing to pipe the shape of a gingerbread boy on top of the cookie sheet. *See H.* Simplify a gingerbread design by piping wavy white detail lines on the head, both arms, and the legs. If you are feeling ambitious, use black detail icing to pipe two dot eyes or a mouth and use red detail icing to pipe his candy buttons. You may have to bust out the PME 1.5 tips here! *See I.*

For heart cookies: Use ivory detail icing to pipe a heart-shaped "cookie" on the cookie sheets. Arrange them on the sheet just as you would when baking cookies on a real cookie sheet, staggered between each other. *See J.* Use light pink detail icing to pipe the "frosting" of the cookie on top of the ivory heart shapes. While the pink icing is still wet, sprinkle your rainbow nonpareils on top. *See K.*

Now that you have seen our favorite cookie sheet designs, what cookie sheets will YOU dream up?!

HO HO HO!!

Santa Claus is coming to town!! Pair these on a tray set out for Santa with some of the Christmas tree cookies (page 111) or reindeer faces (page 108).

Start by preparing your favorite cookie dough from the options on pages 19 to 21 and cutting out as many Santa faces as you would like to decorate! Bake your cookies according to the recipe instructions and let them cool.

Step 1. Outline the furry trim on Santa's hat in white detail icing. This will be a long rectangle shape. Then outline the beard in white, exaggerating the scallops. Outline Santa's hat in red, bringing it to a point at the end of the hat.

Step 2. Use any skin tone to pipe a large U-shape for Santa's face. Allow the outline to dry at least 30 minutes before flooding. *See A.*

Step 3. Flood each section in its matching flood icing color. Let the flood dry for at least 8 hours or overnight before adding top details. *See B.*

Step 4. Use your black food pen to color in a small circle where his mouth will be at the bottom of his face.

Step 5. Using white detail icing, re-outline the beard, adding swirls at both ends for an extra detail. I like to retrace the tip on Santa's hat to make it look clean and finished. Still using white detail icing, pipe a large ball at the end of Santa's hat.

Step 6. Pipe two teardrop shapes for Santa's mustache, bringing them into an upwards point at each end. Pipe two eyebrows in white detail icing.

Step 7. Use black detail icing to pipe two black dots under the eyebrows for his eyes. Using your skin tone color, pipe a dot for a nose right where the mustache meets together.

Step 8. I like to add "Ho Ho Ho" to the top of the hat in light and dark green detail icing! *See C.*

SUPPLIES
Santa face cookie cutter (see Resources, page 185)
Cookie dough (pages 19–21)
Black felt-tip food pen
White sugar crystals (optional)

FLOOD ICING
- Red
- Ivory (or any skin tone)
- White

DETAIL ICING
- White
- Red
- Any skin tone
- Black
- Lime green
- Dark green

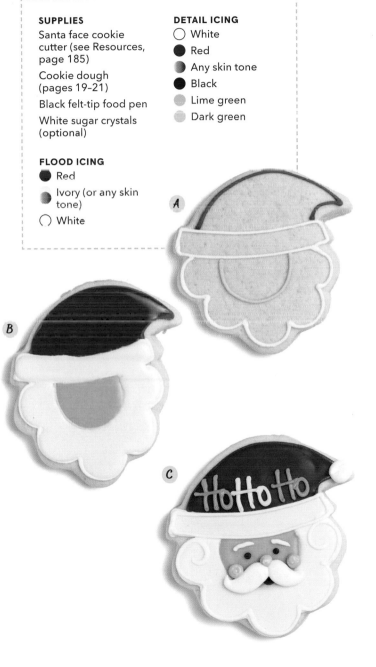

Rudolph the SPRINKLE Nose Reindeer

I'm pretty sure that's how the song goes, right?! You can't go wrong with sprinkles on everything—and what better time than the holidays!

Start by preparing your favorite cookie dough from the options on pages 19 to 21 and cutting out as many reindeer faces as you would like to decorate! Bake your cookies according to the recipe instructions and let them cool.

Step 1. Outline the reindeer face in brown detail icing, rounding the top of the head under the antlers. Pipe a curved line that splits the ears in half. Use light pink detail icing to fill in the bottom half of the ear. *See A.*

Step 2. Outline the antlers in ivory detail icing, squaring off the ends of each branch of the antler into three prongs. Allow the outline to dry at least 30 minutes before flooding.

Step 3. Flood each section in its matching flood color. Let the flood dry for at least 4 hours before moving on to top detail decorations. *See B.*

Step 4. Use red detail icing to pipe a big round circle and fill it in, near the bottom half of the reindeer face. While this icing is still wet, dip the nose in nonpareil sprinkles or red sugar (if using). Or just leave it solid red for a more classic look!

Step 5. Use your edible gold dust and clear alcohol to paint the antlers gold (page 16).

SUPPLIES

Reindeer face cookie cutter (see Resources, page 185)

Cookie dough (pages 19–21)

Rainbow nonpareil sprinkles or red sugar crystals (optional)

White sugar crystals

Gold luster dust and clear alcohol (optional)

Black food pen

DETAIL ICING
- Brown
- Light pink
- Ivory
- Red
- Black
- White

FLOOD ICING
- Brown
- Ivory

A

Step 6. Pipe two black dots for the eyes, adding two smaller white dots on top for the reflection. *See C.*

Step 7. Use a black food pen to pipe a small smile, two light pink cheeks, and three small freckles on either side of the face. Let these details dry for 1 hour, or until crusted over the top and the gold is no longer sticky to the touch.

Step 8. Pipe uneven blobs of white detail icing on top of the ears, antlers, and head to look like snow. While the icing is still wet, dip it in white sugar crystals for the full snowy texture! *See D.*

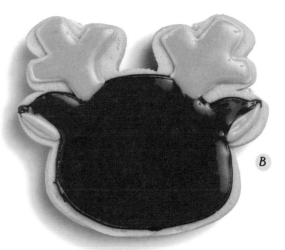
B

C

D

Oh, Christmas Tree!

Christmas tree cookies are some of my favorite to decorate, because you can trim them any way you like! Each year I come up with a new way to design them, and it is so fun to dream up your perfect tree in cookie form. Whether it's rainbow or classy sprinkle garlands, the sky is the limit!

Start by preparing your favorite cookie dough from the options on pages 19 to 21 and cutting out as many Christmas trees as you would like to decorate! I love making our classic gingerbread cookie recipe for these because they are so soft and delicious. All of your guests will be impressed that they taste even better than they look! Bake your cookies according to the recipe instructions and let them cool.

Step 1. Outline the Christmas tree in lime green detail icing, skipping over the base/stump of the tree. Outline the stump in dark brown detail icing. Allow the outline to dry at least 30 minutes before flooding. *See A.*

Step 2. Flood each section in its matching flood color. *See B.*

Continued →

SUPPLIES
Christmas tree cookie cutter (see Resources, page 185)
Cookie dough (pages 19–21)
Sugar crystal sprinkles
Sprinkles

FLOOD ICING
- Lime green
- Dark green
- Brown

DETAIL ICING
- Lime green
- Dark brown
- Dark green
- White
- Colors for details/ rainbow (optional)

A

B

Variation : Sprinkle the entire tree with Christmas sprinkles while the flood icing is still wet. *See C.*

Go back with lime green detail icing—after the flood has set—and draw scalloped lines across each of the three sections of the tree! Stop there, or once the green lines dry, draw three white cascading lines on the tree as a garland, and dip the lines while they are wet in white sugar crystals for a sparkly garland!

Variations

Using rainbow colors, pipe swirly lines like this from bottom to top in rainbow order. These trees could not be any more whimsical if they tried! *See D.*

Pipe three cascading lines in white detail icing and dip them in our favorite winter sprinkle blend of sugar crystals and shimmery rainbow nonpareils. Go back with lime green detail icing to pipe the scalloped sections of the tree. Using rainbow colors or your favorite color, pipe dots for ornaments all over the tree. *See E.*

Pipe scalloped lines in lime green detail icing, separating each section of the tree. On the bottom section of the tree, pipe two large eyes: the bigger they are, the cuter this tree will be! Pipe a small smile between the eyes. Pipe a single, thin black line that slopes diagonally up the tree. Pipe small rainbow dots across the line to act as a string of Christmas lights. Or substitute the dots for a sprinkle dip in a festive Christmas sprinkle mix. *See F.*

I can't wait to see what Christmas tree designs you come up with!

Shut the Front Door!

These front door cookies are the cutest way to say "elcome home." Dress them up for *any* season by changing a few simple details!

Start by preparing your favorite cookie dough from the options on pages 19 to 21 and cutting out as many rectangle shapes as you would like to decorate! Bake your cookies according to the recipe instructions and let them cool.

Step 1. Use your white or red detail icing to outline the rectangle around the edge. Allow to dry for at least 30 minutes before flooding.

Step 2. In the same color as your outline, use your flood icing to fill in the cookie completely. Allow the flood icing to set for 4 hours or overnight, so the details stand out on top of the cookie. *See A.*

Step 3. Pipe two long rectangles that go about one-third of the way down the cookie, starting near the top.

Step 4. Pipe two more long rectangles that take up the bottom two-thirds of the door, underneath the top two rectangles.

Step 5. Use your ivory detail icing to pipe a small round dot, on the right side of the door, between the two rectangles (this is the doorknob!).

Step 6. Mix a little of your gold dust with clear alcohol (page 16). Paint the doorknob gold. Now you have your base "front door" cookie. Here is where you can let your imagination run wild, because you can create your own seasonal wreath to hang front and center! *See B.*

SUPPLIES
Rectangle cookie cutter (see Resources, page 185)
Cookie dough (pages 19-21)
Gold luster dust and clear alcohol

FLOOD ICING
⬤ White or red

DETAIL ICING
⬤ White or red to match the flood
○ Ivory

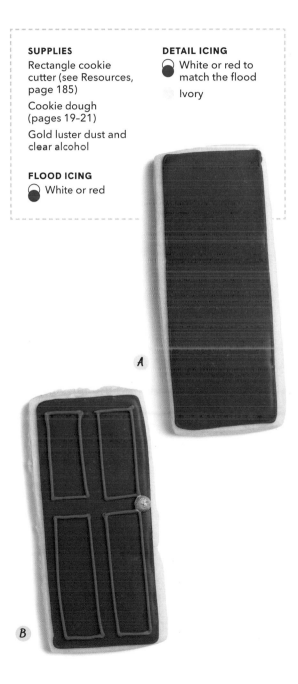

A

B

Christmas Door

Step 1. Use a green detail icing to pipe a dark green wreath. Moving in a circular motion, move the icing back and forth to create a zigzag texture.

Step 2. Use white detail icing to pipe a bow at the bottom of the wreath.

Step 3. Use red detail icing to pipe small holly berries around the wreath, or you can use sprinkles to look like twinkling little rainbow Christmas lights! *See C.*

C

D

Fall Door

Step 1. Use brown detail icing to pipe a wavy line in the shape of a circle.

Step 2. Go back around the wavy line again, with a second line, trying to get between each arch and dip of the wave.

Step 3. Here you can choose your favorite fall colors to create some florals on the bottom of the wreath. (See page 43 for how to pipe a bunch of wiggle flowers.) *See D.*

Spring Door

Follow steps 1 and 2 from the fall door. Add Easter egg sprinkles or a bunny face sprinkle at the bottom of the wreath, or make the flower bunch in pastels. *See E.*

E

What's Crackin'?!

These nutcracker cookies may look intimidating, but don't worry, you're about to be a professional and all of your friends and family will be wondering just how you learned to decorate these *gorgeous* cookies! Pair this in a holiday design with an adorable tray of Christmas trees, some reindeer, or "Merry Christmas!" plaques.

Start by preparing your favorite cookie dough from the options on pages 19 to 21 and cutting out as many nutcracker busts as you would like to decorate! Bake your cookies according to the recipe instructions and let them cool.

Step 1. Outline the nutcracker's hat in light pink detail icing. I skip the bump at the top; this is where his furry "feather" will go. Outline a square for his face in ivory. This shape should only go as far as the tops of the shoulders. *See A.*

Step 2. Outline the two arms in light pink, then connect them at the bottom for his suit. Outline the hair using white detail icing, rounding out three puffs. *See B.*

Step 3. Flood each respective section, letting the section next to it dry before flooding any section that touches each other, so the colors and sections do not bleed together. You want the arms to stand out separately from the body, so you don't have to re-outline them again at the end. Allow the flood to dry for at least 4 hours before moving on to details. *See C on following page.*

Step 4. Pipe a thick line at the base of the hat and a thick squiggly line where the feather portion of the hat would go. While it is still wet, dip both of the lines in sugar crystals.

Step 5. Use a black felt-tip food pen to draw a square at the very bottom of the face. This will be his mouth.

Continued →

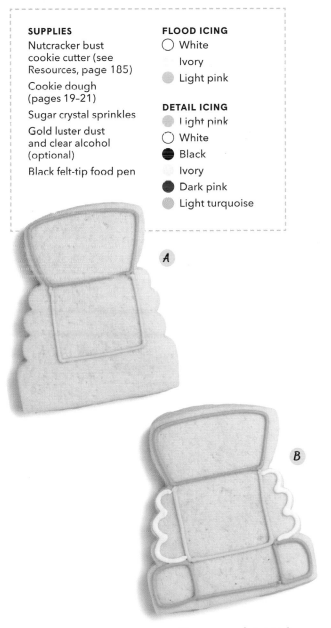

SUPPLIES
Nutcracker bust cookie cutter (see Resources, page 185)
Cookie dough (pages 19–21)
Sugar crystal sprinkles
Gold luster dust and clear alcohol (optional)
Black felt-tip food pen

FLOOD ICING
○ White
　 Ivory
● Light pink

DETAIL ICING
● Light pink
○ White
● Black
　 Ivory
● Dark pink
● Light turquoise

A

B

Step 6. Using white and black detail icing to pipe two eyes, and eyebrows, re-outline the curlycues in the hair and pipe a thick mustache that goes over the top of the food pen mouth you drew. **See D.**

Step 7. Using ivory detail icing, pipe a teardrop nose and a thin line under the square for the bottom lip.

Step 8. With your white detail icing again, pipe a squiggle beard under the bottom lip. Don't dip the beard too low, because you will have his suit fasteners to add in a minute. Use dark pink detail icing to pipe two rosy cheeks.

Step 9. Pipe the shoulder pads using light turquoise detail icing. I do this by arching over the shoulder, following your initial outline, then bringing the shoulder pad down into three dips. Using the light turquoise, pipe small polka dots all over the nutcracker's hat. **See E.**

Step 10. Last but not least, use your ivory detail icing to pipe two small dots for buttons on the nutcracker's chest and connect them with a thin line. When this dries for about 30 minutes, you can paint it using your gold dust and clear alcohol (page 16). **See F.**

Now THAT is a cookie made for a Christmas party!

Change up the skin tones and the suit colors—heck, you can even make it a rainbow nutcracker!

Other Holidays

Champagne Bottle

CHEERS! This preppy little champagne bottle is so dang cute, perfect for a twenty-first birthday, a bachelorette party, or Monday.

Start by preparing your favorite cookie dough from the options on pages 19 to 21 and cutting out as many champagne bottles as you would like to decorate! I will show y'all how to turn this same cutter into a beer bottle (page 123), so cut a few extra so you can make an assortment of alcohol bottles if you are doing a twenty-first birthday or have a beer-lover in your life! Bake your cookies according to the recipe instructions and let them cool.

Step 1. Outline the top of the bottle in ivory detail icing, starting right at the curve of the bottle and forming a V at the bottom. Outline the outside of the bottle in dark green detail icing.

Using light pink detail icing, pipe a rectangular label in the center of the bottle, then add a half-circle on top of the rectangle in the center. Allow the outline to set for at least 1 hour before flooding. *See A.*

Continued →

SUPPLIES

Champagne bottle cookie cutter (see Resources, page 185)

Cookie dough (pages 19–21)

Gold luster dust and clear alcohol (optional)

Champagne Bottle
FLOOD ICING
- ● Dark green
- ● Light pink
- ○ Ivory

DETAIL ICING
- ○ Ivory
- ● Dark green
- ● Light pink
- ● Dark pink
- ○ White

Beer Bottle
FLOOD ICING
- ● Brown
- ● Blue

DETAIL ICING
- ● Brown
- ● Blue
- ○ Ivory
- ○ White

A

Step 2. Flood each section using the respective color. Wait between sections for a cleaner effect, but because you have to re-outline the entire shape, if the colors run together slightly it won't be that big of a deal here. When flooding the light pink section, I flood right over the connecting line between the rectangle and half-circle. Allow the flood to dry for at least 4 hours before adding your top detail decorations. *See B.*

Step 3. Using your gold dust, mix just enough alcohol to make it a paint-like texture and paint the ivory section of your bottle (page 16).

Step 4. Use your white detail icing to re-outline the light pink label. Then add a white highlight detail on the green bottle for a reflective look.

Step 5. Use dark pink detail icing for the ribbon around the bottle! Start by piping a rectangle that follows the line between the gold and the dark green bottle. Pipe two small triangles at the end of the rectangle to create the ribbon-end look. Pipe another of the exact same shape that intersects the first ribbon in the middle.

Step 6. Using light pink detail icing, re-outline the ribbon, making the first ribbon section lie on top of the ribbon below. Here you can add any customization you want, a name, an age, or a simple "Cheers" is the perfect finishing touch! *See C.*

Step 7. Use white detail icing to pipe a few stars and small dots, going up the top of the gold part.

B

C

Beer Bottle

Now to turn this cutter into a beer bottle. Only a few color swaps will do it!

Step 1. Use a royal blue detail icing (or any color you want for the beer label), to pipe a rectangle in the middle of the bottle shape, for the label. Using brown detail icing, trace the rest of the outside of the bottle. Allow the outline to dry for at least 1 hour before flooding. *See D.*

Step 2. Using your royal blue flood icing and brown flood icing, flood the sections with their respective color. Allow the flood to dry for at least 4 hours before moving on to top detail decorations. *See E.*

Step 3. Use ivory detail icing to pipe a bottle cap on top: Pipe one thick, straight line at the very top of the bottle. Return to the bottom of that line and add a wiggly line.

Step 4. Use white detail icing to go back and add the reflective line to the beer bottle.

Step 5. For the label you can try to replicate your favorite beer logo. Or write a witty "BEer Mine" on the label for your valentine or "Cheers and beers to 30 years" for a thirtieth birthday! So many options, so little time!

Step 6. When your bottle cap has dried, paint the bottle cap gold or silver (page 16) if you want the extra pop of metallic color. *See F.*

From here, get creative and turn this into a vodka or tequila bottle –almost any alcohol bottle you want can be made with this cutter!

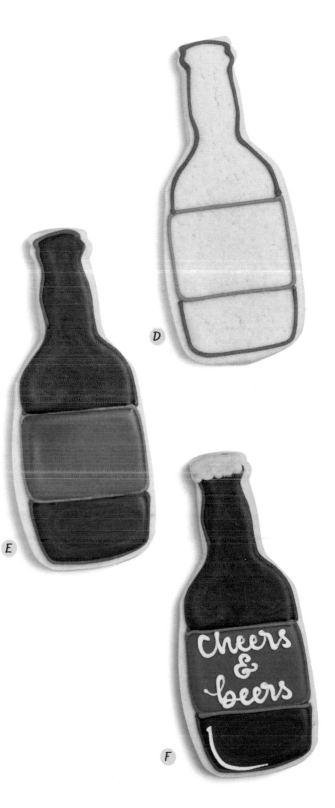

Champagne Flute

Cheers! We all have that *one* story of when we drank too much. Mine may have involved a four loco and a bathroom floor. But let's pretend I was classy and it was a champagne hangover, ha-ha! But you know what will never do ya dirty like that? COOKIES! Whether you are celebrating New Year's, a wedding toast, or even a birthday party, these champagne flute cookies are just fancy enough to make your party feel classy as all get out. And no hangover—guaranteed!

Start by preparing your favorite cookie dough from the options on pages 19 to 21 and cutting out as many flute shapes as you would like to decorate! You can't go wrong with a classic sugar cookie. After all, we are trying to keep it classy! Bake your cookies according to the recipe instructions and let them cool.

Step 1. Using the white detail icing, start at the top left corner and draw a straight line down, creating a point in the center of the base. Then go back up to the other corner—like drawing an upside-down triangle. You want this outlined in white, even though you won't flood it white. This will make it look like the glass part of the champagne flute. *See A.*

Step 2. Outline the bottom of the glass in white, cinching in a little bit then rounding it out at the bottom. Allow the outline to set for about 30 minutes before flooding for the cleanest results; this way it sets up hard enough to hold the glaze icing inside without chipping away.

Note: This cookie uses a wet-on-wet technique for the bubbles of the champagne, so work quickly. Be sure not to flood too many at the same time when you flood the ivory.

Continued →

SUPPLIES	FLOOD ICING
Champagne flute cookie (see Resources, page 185)	⬜ Ivory
	⚪ White
Cookie dough (pages 19–21)	**DETAIL ICING**
Tip number 3	⚪ White
Gold edible glitter dust	
Sugar crystal sprinkles	

A

Step 3. Flood the top section in ivory glaze. While it is still wet, use a tip number 3 on your white flood bottle to create bubbles. Start with a bigger dot (squeeze harder), then do two more smaller dots above the bigger dot. I like to add three sets of three dots on the cookie. One at the bottom, one on the right side, and one at the top. **See B.**

Step 4. Flood the bottom of the flute in white. Allow the cookie to dry for at least 8 hours, or until you can touch the cookie without it denting/sticking to your finger. **See C.**

Step 5. Pipe a line across the top of the glass using your white detail icing. Then make bigger drop-lets on the right side that gradually get smaller as you work your way back to the left. While this icing is still wet, dip this into the sugar crystals. This will give you a 3-D bubble effect and it is oh so sparkly! **See D.**

Cheers!! You're ready to celebrate in style!

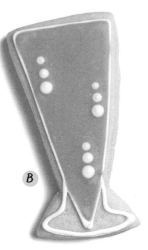

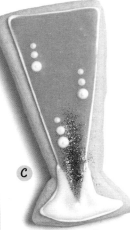

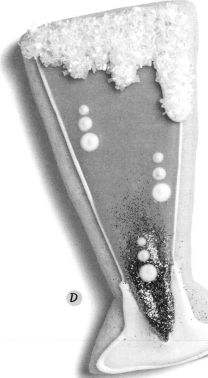

Disco Ball Cookies

Ring in the new year with these sparkly disco ball cookies! After all, it's not really a party without a disco ball. These simple, stunning cookies will jazz up any celebration.

Start by preparing your favorite cookie dough from the options on pages 19 to 21 and cutting out as many shapes as you would like to decorate! Bake your cookies according to the recipe instructions and let them cool.

Step 1. Use gray detail icing to outline a circle around the top edge of the round cookie. *See A.*

Step 2. Use your gray flood icing to fill in the cookie. Note: The next steps are done while the flood icing is still wet, so work as quickly as you can. It is not imperative that it is done wet on wet: we find that if you wait and do the next steps when the flood icing is dry, it is more likely that the detail icing on top will flake off when it is dry. This technique also allows you to write on top of the disco ball to add a year or name! *See B.*

Step 3. While the flood icing is still wet, paint it with silver icing. Immediately dust the silver lightly with sparkly edible glitter! You don't want to taste or feel the texture of this glitter when you bite into the cookie, so a little goes a long way! *See C.*

Continued →

SUPPLIES
Round cookie cutter
Cookie dough
(pages 19–21)
Tip number 2
Silver edible glitter
Silver edible paint

FLOOD ICING
● Gray

DETAIL ICING
● Black
● Gray

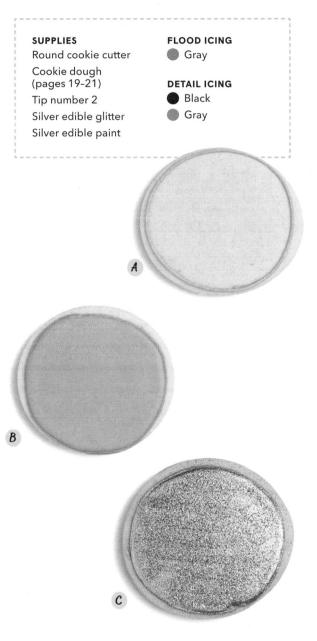

Step 4. Trace the round outline of the cookie in black detail icing. Start by piping a straight black line, vertically down the center of the round cookie. *See D.* Then add slightly arched vertical lines on either side. *See E.* Starting at the top, pipe slightly arched U-shapes in black, working your way down the cookie.

Step 5. To take these cookies to the next level, try adding a year, a name, or some cheeky writing on it! Happy New Year!

Now—BOOM! You are ready to kiss your date at midnight—or maybe sub the date for these cookies!

You're PURRRfect, Cat Face Valentine

I know that you know a cat lady. Maybe you ARE the cat lady. I suggest pairing these with some cute plaque shapes that read "You're purrrrfect" or "I love you and I ain't KITTEN you!"

Start by preparing your favorite cookie dough from the options on pages 19 to 21 and cutting out as many cat face cookies as you would like to decorate! Bake your cookies according to the recipe instructions and let them cool.

Step 1. Outline the white part of the cat face: we want this cat to have a white ear and one white eye patch. Start by outlining the white of the ear along the edge of the cookie, then dipping down to cover the area that the right eye would be in.

Step 2. Use your orange detail icing to outline the remainder of the cat face, using the edge of the cookie as your guide. Allow the outline to set up at least 30 minutes before flooding for the cleanest result. *See A.*

Step 3. Flood the white part of the cat face. I recommend immediately flooding the orange as well instead of letting the white set, because you want the two colors to run together slightly to create a smooth finish. Allow the flood to set at least 4 hours or overnight. You will be using food pen on these cookies; the icing needs to harden so you don't make a hole in the cookie. If you do not have time to wait for the icing to get this hard, forgo the food pen and pipe the lines in black detail icing.

Continued →

Continued →

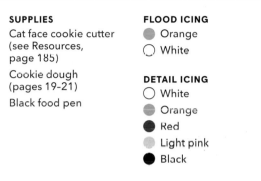

SUPPLIES
Cat face cookie cutter (see Resources, page 185)
Cookie dough (pages 19-21)
Black food pen

FLOOD ICING
● Orange
○ White

DETAIL ICING
○ White
● Orange
● Red
● Light pink
● Black

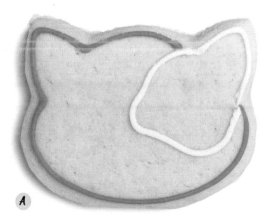

A

Step 4. Use the red detail icing to pipe hearts around where the eyes would go. These will be glasses for the kitty! If you need to, use a food pen to lightly sketch out the heart shapes before piping the icing on. Just know you will have to try and cover the food pen up after it is done!

Step 5. Connect the hearts with a small line across the bridge of the nose and two lines to the edge of the face to complete the glasses.

Step 6. Use a food pen to give the cat smiley eyelash eyes, whiskers, and a little mouth. *See B.*

Step 7. Use the light pink to pipe a small heart for the nose.

Note : How to pipe a heart: Start by squeezing a round dot. While the tip of your piping bag is still in the dot, lighten up on the squeeze and pull toward you, creating a teardrop shape. Repeat this next to the other dot, connecting the two teardrops to create a heart!

Step 8. If you have extra icing, you can add a flower crown to the top of this cute cat's head—or even a drip of icing and sprinkles!! *See C.*

B

C

Love Notes

Take yourself back to grade school with these cookies—which I would much rather receive than a folded piece of notebook paper! Just don't throw it across the room in airplane form. It won't end well. These would be perfect for the first day of school for a new teacher or in your kiddo's lunchbox for a sweet treat!

Start by preparing your favorite cookie dough from the options on pages 19 to 21 and cutting out as many hearts as you would like to decorate! Bake your cookies according to the recipe instructions and let them cool.

Step 1. Outline the entire heart in white detail icing. *See A.* Allow the outline to dry for at least 30 minutes, then flood with white flood icing. Let the flood dry for 8 hours or overnight. This design uses food pen so make sure the icing is completely dry!

Step 2. Using a ruler or the edge of a sheet of paper, trace lines in blue food pen horizontally down the heart. (Think lines on a sheet of notebook paper.) Leave about an inch of blank space at the top, just like paper!

Step 3. Draw a straight vertical line in red food pen down the left side of the heart. *See B.* I like to use red detail icing to write a big A+ at the top right-hand side of the heart. (Maybe wishful thinking, but bribing a teacher with these cookies can't hurt, right?!)

Step 4. Use black food pen or black detail icing to write "Good luck with my kid!" or "Have a great first day!" It would even be fun to give your kid a food pen and have them write their own message to a teacher on these! *See C.*

SUPPLIES	FLOOD ICING
Heart cookie cutter (or any shape!)	○ White
Cookie dough (pages 19-21)	**DETAIL ICING**
Blue food pen	○ White
Red food pen	● Red
Black food pen (optional)	● Black

Little Bunny

This little bunny has so many ways you can dress him up! The Easter bunny ain't got nothin' on this cutie!

Start by preparing your favorite cookie dough from the options on pages 19 to 21 and cutting out as many bunny body shapes as you would like to decorate! Try mixing in some pastel sprinkles to your dough, to make them festive for spring. Bake your cookies according to the recipe instructions and let them cool.

Step 1. Outline the bunny body in pastel purple detail icing, rounding out the bottom near the tail. You can leave this un-outlined because you will be adding the tail last! Allow the outline to set for at least 30 minutes for the cleanest results. *See A.*

Step 2. Using a tip 12, flood the entire bunny with the pastel purple flood icing. Allow the flood icing to dry for at least 4 hours or overnight so the sprinkles only stick to the tail when it is dipped.

Step 3. Add a small pastel pink heart on the tip of the bunny nose and two long teardrops for the bunny's ears. I do this by starting at the tip with a large dot, dragging the tip down as I continue to squeeze and let up on the pressure slowly. *See B.*

Step 4. You can use either a simple black dot for the bunny's eye or make a swoopy eye with eyelashes for a slightly fancier look.

Step 5. Here is where you can get creative with it!

Variations

Add a sweet little bow around the neck using the white detail icing. *See C.*

Add a flower crown to the top of the bunny head, or use the same flowers to wrap around the bunny's neck like an adorable spring wreath! (See page 43 for how to create these wiggle flowers that can jazz up ANY design!) *See D.*

SUPPLIES
Bunny body cookie cutter (see Resources, page 185)
Cookie dough (pages 19-21)
White nonpareil sprinkles
Tip number 12

FLOOD ICING
● Pastel purple

DETAIL ICING
● Pastel purple
● Pastel pink
● Black
○ White

Dia de los Muertos Sugar Skulls

Spooky or cute? You decide! Change up the colors to create a more fun vibe, or go all dark using black and white for a creepier feel! It's all about the details for these intricate cookies—the more you add, the more impressive they become!

Start by preparing your favorite cookie dough from the options on pages 19 to 21 and cutting out as many skull shapes as you would like to decorate! Bake your cookies according to the recipe instructions and let them cool.

Step 1. Outline the skull cookie along the edge in a white detail icing. *See A.*

Step 2. Flood the cookie with a white flood icing. Fill all the holes so you don't end up with more unnecessary holes in the head than you already have! Allow the icing to develop a crust, or completely dry if you have the time. *See B.*

Step 3. From here on, only use your detail icing. I like to start with the eyes, as they are the window to the cookie soul. Use the ivory detail icing to pipe hearts where the eyes should be, just above the cheekbones. I usually start by outlining the heart, then fill it in. You can use a toothpick or the end of the piping bag to wiggle the icing around until it is somewhat smooth. *See C on following page.*

Step 4. Use black icing to pipe the outline of the mouth. Start with a curlycue shape and make a U, with the two curlycues curving under at either side.

Continued →

SUPPLIES
Skull cookie cutter (see Resources, page 185)
Cookie dough (pages 19–21)
Gold luster dust and clear alcohol

FLOOD ICING
○ White

DETAIL ICING
As many as your hands can mix!
I recommend:
○ White
  Ivory
● Red
● Orange
  Yellow
● Lime green
● Dark turquoise
  Light turquoise
● Dark purple
● Hot pink
● Black

A

B

Step 5. Add the top curlycue line by making the curlycue curve upwards, then a straight line, connecting the bottom U to the top with more curly ends.

Step 6. Still using black, pipe a tiny upside-down heart between the eyes and above the mouth for a nose! *See D.*

Step 7. Fill in each "tooth" with a different color. I like to go in rainbow order to keep that vibe going, but you could mix these up, use all one color, or come up with your own color scheme. Try different shades of pink for a fun girly look, or how about fifty shades of gray?!

Step 8. This is the time to let your creative side shine and add details for a cool sugar skull! Dots, lines, squiggles, swirls, you name it! For these, I start with a thick V-shape going from the top of the skull to the middle of the eyes.

Step 9. I add a thinner V-line in a different color, above the first V. Add a row of tiny dots above the V. Add a row of teardrops below the bottom V, pointing upward. *See E.*

Step 10. *Go crazy!* Use the gold dust luster and clear alcohol on the heart-shaped eyes. Add more dots, more swirls—more, more, more! Until you have them exactly how you want them. And hey, maybe less is more for you. And that's fine too, I won't judge ya . . . too hard. *See F.*

What is so fun about these cookies is if you don't want to do heart eyes, you could do stars or flowers or whatever else your heart could dream up!

Fabulous Jack-o-lantern Cookies

These aren't your average jack-o-lanterns. We have taken it up 100 notches by adding the gold sparkle behind the eyes, like they are actually glowing! They look magically haunted and will impress for *any* Halloween party!

Start by preparing your favorite cookie dough from the options on pages 19 to 21 and cutting out as many pumpkins as you would like to decorate! These would be fun to switch up between multiple pumpkin shapes, just like real life. Or pair these with cute ghosts (page 145) or even a cute BOO plaque! Bake your cookies according to the recipe instructions and let them cool.

Step 1. Start by painting the center of your pumpkin cookie with your gold dust (page 16). Try not to paint any gold on the outer centimeter of the cookie. Then sprinkle a little edible gold glitter (if using). I think it adds a nice sparkly touch! *See A.*

Step 2. Using your orange detail icing, start at the top center of the pumpkin (skipping the stem) and outline around the entire outer edge of the pumpkin shape. Still using your orange detail icing, pipe two triangles for eyes. Remember you will NOT be filling in the center of these, so keep any extra icing outside of these holes.

Continued →

SUPPLIES	FLOOD ICING
Pumpkin cookie cutter (see Resources, page 185)	● Brown
	● Orange
Cookie dough (pages 19-21)	**DETAIL ICING**
Gold luster dust and clear alcohol	● Orange
	● Brown
Edible gold glitter (optional)	● Dark green

A

Step 3. Pipe a smaller triangle for the nose, between the eye triangles. Pipe the mouth by piping a line that curves slightly downward and dips down into a triangular point, then finish out the top line of the smile. Finish the bottom line of the smile with two triangular points on either side of the top tooth.

Step 4. Use your brown detail icing to pipe the outline of the stem. Let the outline set for 1 hour. *See B.*

Step 5. Flood the orange part of the pumpkin with orange glaze. Use a smaller tip when necessary to avoid getting any icing in the holes of the eyes, nose, or mouth. *See C.* Flood the stem brown with glaze icing.

Step 6. Almost done with this fabulously spooky pumpkin! Take your dark green detail icing and pipe a swirly vine coming down the top side of the jack-o-lantern. To make it even fancier, try substituting the orange pumpkin for a white pumpkin base. Or get funky with rainbow pumpkins! *See D.*

B

C

D

Fall Leaf

This design is beautiful and simply made. The decorating is done with the flood icing, so you don't have to wait for it to set up to have a perfectly finished cookie! Pair this with some classic fall pumpkins or funny fall quotes and you will have the perfect autumn cookie platter.

Start by preparing your favorite cookie dough from the options on pages 19 to 21 and cutting out as many fall leaves as you would like to decorate! How fun would it be to mix up the shapes of the leaves for an assorted look. Bake your cookies according to the recipe instructions and let them cool.

Step 1. Using your brown detail icing, outline around the edge of the leaf cookie. Allow the outline to dry for at least 30 minutes before moving on to flooding. *See A.*

Step 2. Using a tip 10 or smaller on all of your flood bottles, start with a thin outline of brown flood icing. This design is wet on wet, so work fast and don't flood too many cookies at the same time. *See B.*

Step 3. Follow the same shape of the brown icing and working in like concentric circles. Use your red icing for the next layer.

Step 4. Flood the next concentric outline with orange, then yellow. *See C.*

Step 5. Now for the soothing part: If you are into ASMR, grab your phone and put this on Instagram. Using a toothpick, drag the tip through all of the colors, in and out, making the colors swirl together however you wish! *See D.*

Step 6. Optional: I always like to add a little shimmer to the edges of my fall leaves! Dip a small paintbrush into the edible glitter and tap it along the edges of the cookie, or all over if you want it really sparkly. *See E.*

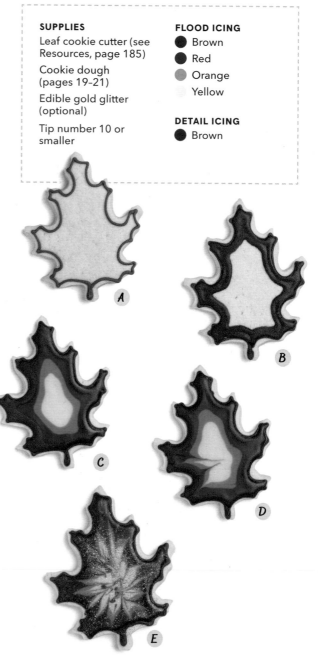

SUPPLIES
Leaf cookie cutter (see Resources, page 185)
Cookie dough (pages 19-21)
Edible gold glitter (optional)
Tip number 10 or smaller

FLOOD ICING
● Brown
● Red
● Orange
○ Yellow

DETAIL ICING
● Brown

Hallo-WEENIE Dog Cookies

Because who doesn't love a cute puppy ready to jump out and scare ya!

Start by preparing your favorite cookie dough from the options on pages 19 to 21 and cutting out as many dachshund cookies as you would like to decorate. To get in the spirit of Halloween, you could dye the cookie dough orange or add pumpkin spice flavor! Bake your cookies according to the recipe instructions and let them cool.

Step 1. Using your white detail icing, outline the top of the dachshund's head and ears, making the distinction between the head and the ears. Use a wavy line, just above the lower belly of the dog, following up the tail and connecting it back to the ears.

Step 2. Using your brown detail icing, pipe two circles for the dog's eyes. Fill them in with the detail icing. Outline both front paws, and the back two paws, connecting the brown line to the white of the sheet. Allow the outline to set up for at least 30 minutes before flooding. *See A.*

Step 3. Using your white flood icing, fill in the white of the sheet, being careful to flood around the eyes and not cover them up. You can use a toothpick for more precision around the eyes or if you are afraid of your flood bottle touching the eyes.

Step 4. Using your brown flood icing, fill in the bottom of the dog you outlined in brown. Allow the flood to set for at least 4 hours or overnight. *See B.*

Step 5. Using your white detail icing, retrace the head separately from the ears. Then re-outline the bottom of the sheet adding small vertical lines, coming up from the wavy line to create the effect of a fold or ruffle in the sheet. Add two black eyes on top of the brown eye holes you piped earlier and a black dot for a nose on the end of the "head" outline. Using your brown detail icing, outline the front and back legs that are furthest to the right, making it look like one leg is in front and one is in back. *See C.*

SUPPLIES	DETAIL ICING
Dachshund cookie cutter (see Resources, page 185)	○ White
	● Brown
	● Black
Cookie dough (pages 19–21)	

FLOOD ICING
○ White
● Chocolate brown

Lollipop Ghost

These ghosts are perfect for spooky season or for your friend who just got ghosted! These would look SO cute in a chocolate cookie dough, making the white ghost really POP. Or add them to a party tray full of other Halloween cookies!

Start by preparing your favorite cookie dough from the options on pages 19 to 21 and cutting out as many ghost cookies as you would like to decorate! Bake your cookies according to the recipe instructions and let them cool.

Step 1. Outline the entire shape in white detail icing. Allow the outline to set up for at least 30 minutes. *See A.* Flood the entire shape solid white with glaze icing. Allow the flood icing to dry for at least 4 hours before moving on to the top details. *See B.*

Step 2. Using detail icing, pipe two big black eyes near the top of the ghost and a tiny U-shaped mouth. Add the white dots on the black eyes to make them a little more cutesy!

Step 3. Pipe two light pink cheeks. Pipe two white arms, just like we did on the paulette bear cookie (page 57). These are just long U-shapes that slant diagonally down toward the belly.

Step 4. Pipe a dark pink line for the lollipop stick in the ghost's hand. Do this by piping two small lines, one on top of the hand and one on the bottom of the hand.

Step 5. Use our tutorial on page 28 for how to create rainbow unicorn poo icing. Put a tip 8 on the unicorn poo icing, and starting in the middle, swirl slowly around, multiple times, building the circle outward. *See C.*

If you don't have this exact ghost shape, you can use ANY ghost shape and simply cut the arms off before baking it. Or leave the arms on and decorate the ghost holding a string of lights!

SUPPLIES
Ghost cookie cutter (see Resources, page 185)
Cookie dough (pages 19-21)
Tip number 8

FLOOD ICING
○ White

DETAIL ICING
○ White
● Black
● Light pink
● Dark pink
◑ Unicorn poo

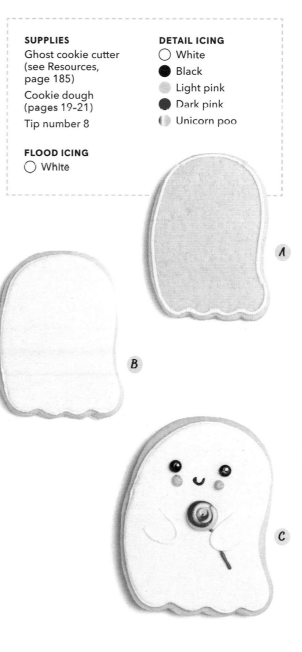

Make a Wish!!

This is one of my favorite designs for when you have leftover cookies. It looks great on any shape. It is SO festive and fun, and it gets you in the birthday spirit! Match your colors to an existing set or come up with a fun new color palette! Make a complete set of cookies by adding these in with a few of our present stack cookies from page 148!

Start by preparing your favorite cookie dough from the options on pages 19 to 21 and cutting out as many plaque-shaped cookies as you would like to decorate! Bake your cookies according to the recipe instructions and let them cool.

Step 1. Outline the plaque in white detail icing. **See A.** Let that dry for at least 30 minutes before flooding with white flood icing. Because we are using a food pen on this design, allow the cookie to dry for at least 8 hours or overnight for the best results!

Step 2. When you have your color palette chosen and prepped, pipe straight lines that go from the bottom of the cookie to about halfway up. I am working in rainbow order with a tip number 3 fitted on my piping bag. (Use a smaller tip for smaller candles, if you wish.) **See B.**

Step 3. Use black detail icing to pipe small black lines on top of each candle for the wick.

Pipe teardrop shapes (like the leaves of a flower), pointing upwards in ivory detail icing. Let the icing dry for at least 30 minutes, then go pack and paint the ivory flames with gold luster dust (page 16).

Step 4. In black food pen, write a scripty "happy birthday" message at the top. Classic! **See C.**

SUPPLIES
Long plaque cookie cutter or any shape! (see Resources, page 185)

Cookie dough (pages 19-21)

Tip number 3, plus smaller tips for candles

Gold luster dust and clear alcohol

Black food pen

FLOOD ICING
○ White

DETAIL ICING
ANY! We will be using rainbow here!

● Black

Ivory

Stacks on Stacks on Stacks

. . . of presents that is!! Make these cookies for a birthday or Christmas celebration. This is one of those fun designs you can decorate any way you want to—and those are the funnest ones! Pair these with a sweet "happy birthday!" plaque for the perfect personalized gift.

Start by preparing your favorite cookie dough from the options on pages 19 to 21 and cutting out as many present stacks as you would like to decorate! Bake your cookies according to the recipe instructions and let them cool.

Step 1. We will work our way from the top down on this design. Start by outlining the top box of the present light turquoise. Outline the middle box light pink and the bottom box dark turquoise. Using dark pink, outline the shape of the bow at the top. Then draw a vertical rectangle for the bow ribbon on the first box. Let the outline dry for at least 30 minutes. *See A.*

Step 2. Flood each section with its matching color. When flooding the dark pink bow, I flood right over the light turquoise line from the first present box; you don't want it to show anyway! I did not do any wet on wet for this design, but now would be the perfect time to do polka dots if you wanted to! Let the flood dry for at least 4 hours before continuing to top details. *See B.*

SUPPLIES
Triple present stack cookie cutter with bow (see Resources, page 185)
Cookie dough (pages 19–21)

FLOOD ICING
● Dark pink
● Light pink
● Light turquoise
● Dark turquoise

DETAIL ICING
● Light turquoise
● Light pink
● Dark turquoise
● Dark pink

A

Step 3. Using dark pink detail icing, re-outline the bow. Start by outlining the center round part of the bow, then both sides. I like to draw two small lines to look like wrinkles in the bow, coming out of the center circle.

Step 4. From here you can add as many or as few details as you would like. I like to pipe large dots on the bottom present in a dark pink detail icing and smaller dots on the top present in dark turquoise detail icing. Add a swirly center down the middle of the middle present! **See C.**

Variations

Make the entire cookie white with a big red bow, then add rainbow details on top like polka dots or chevron stripes!

Use red and green colors to make a Christmas present stack, flooding the middle present white and using red icing to pipe diagonal lines—like a candy cane!

Add a name to the middle present for a custom birthday gift!

Summer Fun

Tie-Dye Shirt Cookies

The tie-dye trend is IN and we all know it! The funnest thing about these cookies is you can switch up the pattern or the colors to create your very own brand of tie-dye with this easy technique! These would also be fun on ANY shape, not just T-shirts. Try making a tie-dye birthday cake cookie or a present shape!

Start by preparing your favorite cookie dough from the options on pages 19 to 21 and cutting out as many T-shirt shaped cookies as you would like to decorate! Bake your cookies according to the recipe instructions and let them cool.

Step 1. Using your red detail icing color, outline the shape of the T-shirt. If you are switching colors up, just outline with the color you want to be the first flood color you use. Allow the outline to dry at least 1 hour before flooding. The rest of this design is done using a wet-on-wet technique, so remember to work quickly and not do too many cookies at the same time. *See A.*

Step 2. Using your red flood icing fitted with a tip 10 or smaller, pipe a thin layer of flood following the outer edge of the T-shirt only. *See B.* Using the colors in rainbow order, orange, yellow, green, blue, and purple (or whatever color combo you want to do), work in concentric T-shirt shapes, gradually getting smaller as you work toward the middle of the T-shirt shape. Make sure the icing touches the color that went before it.

Continued →

SUPPLIES	DETAIL ICING
T-shirt cookie cutter (see Resources, page 185)	● Red
	○ White
Cookie dough (pages 19–21)	**FLOOD ICING**
Toothpicks	● Red
Tip number 10 or smaller	● Orange
	Yellow
	● Lime green
	● Dark turquoise
	● Dark purple

A

B

Step 3. Here is the super satisfying part!! Take a clean toothpick and run it in and out of the icing, like a starburst motion, blending the colors all together just like a tie-dye shirt! *See C and D.*

Variation: For a different pattern, after outlining the initial outer shape, start with a spiral and build the rest of your colors around that spiral. When you move the toothpick through that, it will look more like a spirograph, hypnotizing pattern!

Variation: For a third pattern, pipe horizontal lines in your flood icing one after the other. Then run your toothpick from top to bottom, then bottom to top!

Step 4. Allow the flood icing to set for at least 4 hours or overnight before writing anything on top. Using white detail icing, I like to go back and write a fun message on top: "Stay weird" or "Peace, love, tie-dye" are fun. Heck, even a "Happy Birthday" message would be the perfect finishing touch! *See E.*

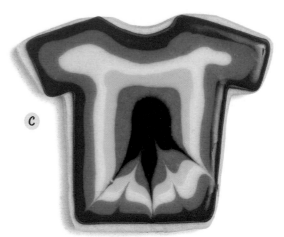

C

D

E

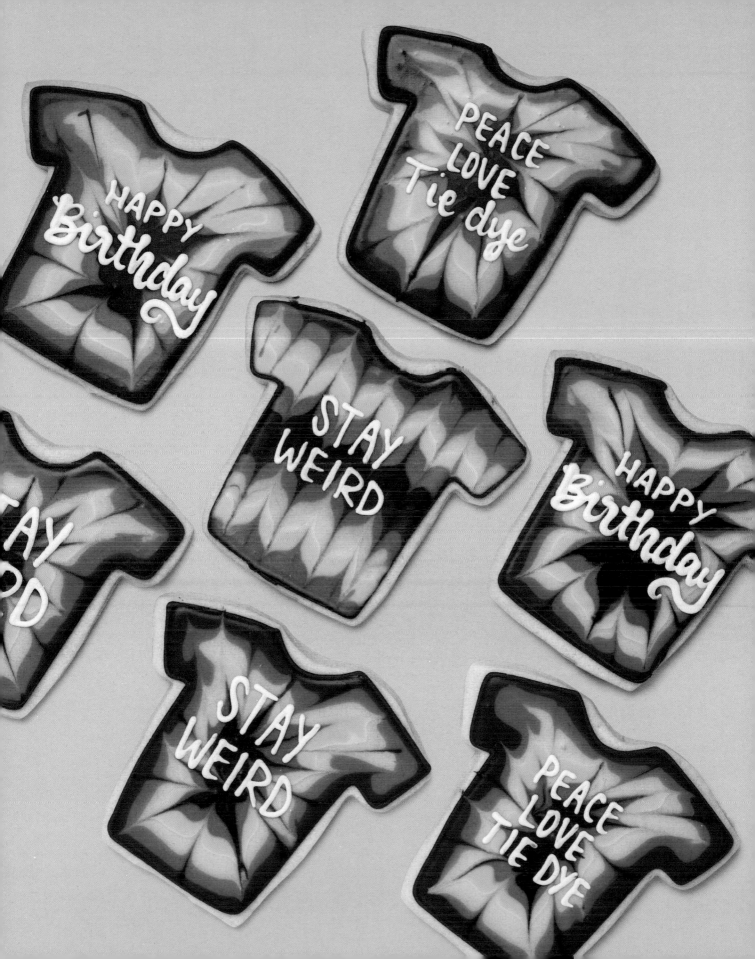

The Fanciest Seashells

These cookies look so real you won't want to eat them! I made these for my grandmother once about seven years ago and she still has them in her china cabinet. Yes, seriously—and once you make them you will see why! Maybe the best part of this design: you only need white icing to make them, so no endless hours of color mixing before you can start!

Start by preparing your favorite cookie dough from the options on pages 19 to 21 and cutting out as many seashells as you would like to decorate! Bake your cookies according to the recipe instructions and let them cool.

Step 1. Outline the entire seashell in white detail icing. Pipe a line down the right side of the shell to divide the "inside of the shell" from the outside. I like to make this slightly curved and wavy, just like the natural edge of a seashell. Allow the outline to dry for at least 30 minutes before flooding. *See A.*

Step 2. Flood the "inner" part of the shell first with white flood icing. While the icing is still wet, dip it in your sprinkle mix. Brush off any extra sprinkles that may be stuck to the cookie in the wrong place.

Step 3. Flood the other side of the seashell. Use a toothpick to pick out any sprinkles that may get stuck in the "outside" of the seashell, as you want it to be clean and smooth. Allow the flood to dry for about 4 hours before moving on to top details. *See B.*

Step 4. Pipe a few curved lines near the top of the shell in white detail icing. Retrace the line between the sprinkles and the smooth side. Pipe a diagonal line on the shell. Add small white dots along all of the lines. *See C.*

SUPPLIES
Seashell cookie cutter (see Resources, page 185)
Cookie dough (pages 19-21)
Under the Sea sprinkle mix
Silver airbrush sheen coloring
Airbrush

FLOOD ICING
○ White

DETAIL ICING
○ White

A

B

C

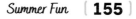

Mermaids!!!

Okay, if you know anything about our bakery, you know that we do an annual "mermaid week." Each summer, we turn the most outrageous things into mermaids! Bacon mermaids, joe exotic mermaids, panda mermaids . . . you name it! This section is meant to get your brain turning, so I can see all of your funny mermaid ideas come to life!! Get silly with it! Pair these with some seashells (page 155), starfish, or a calligraphy cookie like "we mer-made for each other!"

Start by preparing your favorite cookie dough from the options on pages 19 to 21 and cutting out as many mermaids as you would like to decorate! Bake your cookies according to the recipe instructions and let them cool. Let's start off with your basic mermaid and branch off from there.

Step 1. Outline the tail in dark purple detail icing. Start that tail low enough to be sure that you have room for her seashell bra on top!

Step 2. Outline the hair using hot pink detail icing. I do this by making a "curtain" shape near the top of the head and rounding it out on top. I then pipe two small buns where the cat ears would have been! Pipe a large dot, then continue squeezing the icing into a spiral on top of that dot of icing.

Step 3. Outline the head, neck, arms, and body in your skin color of choice. It can be hard to guess where the neck should be, so if you are lacking confidence to freehand this, grab your brown food pen and lightly sketch it out on the cookie first! Allow the outline to set for at least 30 minutes before flooding. **See A.**

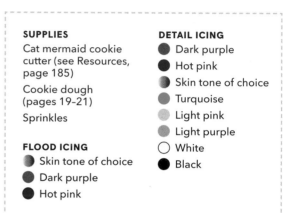

SUPPLIES
Cat mermaid cookie cutter (see Resources, page 185)
Cookie dough (pages 19–21)
Sprinkles

FLOOD ICING
● Skin tone of choice
● Dark purple
● Hot pink

DETAIL ICING
● Dark purple
● Hot pink
● Skin tone of choice
● Turquoise
● Light pink
● Light purple
○ White
● Black

_A_

Step 4. Flood each section in its coordinating flood color. I like to start with the tail because it gets sprinkles wet on wet. If you do that first, your sprinkles can't get stuck in the other colors!

My favorite sprinkles to use are this "under the sea" sprinkle mix you can find on our website! Allow the flood icing to dry for at least 4 hours. **See B.**

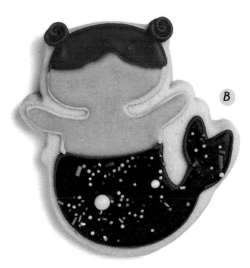

Step 5. Start by piping two open eyes, using black and white detail icing. I like to add eyelashes on my mermaids!

Step 6. Use your skin tone detail icing to pipe a small dot for the nose.

Step 7. Using light pink detail icing, pipe a small heart for her lips. You can also just use your black detail icing and draw a simple smile, if you prefer!

Step 8. Re-outline the hair in hot pink detail icing and add two eyebrows in the matching hair color!

Step 9. Pipe a small starfish in the light purple in her hair, and while the icing is still wet use a tiny pinch of sprinkles to put on top of the starfish! **See C.**

Step 10. Re-outline the top of the tail. I like to add a simple scallop underneath the line, using a light purple detail icing.

Step 11. Pipe two clamshells for her bra using the turquoise detail icing! You can do this by drawing five teardrop shapes, side by side, making the middle one the largest, and getting gradually smaller on both sides. Connect the two clamshells with a line.

Now that you have your standard mermaid design mastered, you can get creative!

Rainbow Flowers!

These rainbow petal flowers are perfect whether you go with bright and vibrant or pastel and soft. They are wonderful for spring or Mother's Day! Try these with the megafetti sprinkled cookie dough because they are full of color. Pairing with an all white plaque with a script name or "love you" message would also look so beautiful together.

Start by preparing your favorite cookie dough from the options on pages 19 to 21 and cutting out as many flowers as you would like to decorate! Bake your cookies according to the recipe instructions and let them cool.

Step 1. Going in rainbow order, outline each of the six petals in a different color. Start in the very center of the flower, piping a teardrop shape in dark pink—then orange next to that, then yellow, lime green, dark turquoise, and dark purple. Allow the outline to set up for at least 1 hour before flooding. *See A.*

Step 2. You can flood the petals simultaneously because the petals are just barely touching the outlines. Using your glaze icing, flood each petal with its respective flood color. Allow the icing to dry for at least 4 hours before moving on to the top details.

Step 3. Pipe a swirl on every petal in detail icing in the same color as the flood. Starting at the pointy part of each petal, pipe a line going up that curls in a spiral at the fat part of the petal. Do this on every petal. *See B.*

Step 4. For the center of the flower, use white detail icing to pipe a large white round circle and fill it all in with the detail icing. Pipe a swirly white spiral on top of the blob! *See C.*

You can swap out any colors for the petals. The pastel colors are the cutest for an Easter cookie tray!

SUPPLIES
Six-petal flower cookie cutter (see Resources, page 185)
Cookie dough (pages 19–21)

FLOOD ICING
- Dark pink
- Orange
- Yellow
- Lime green
- Dark turquoise
- Dark purple

DETAIL ICING
- Dark pink
- Orange
- Yellow
- Lime green
- Dark turquoise
- Dark purple
- White

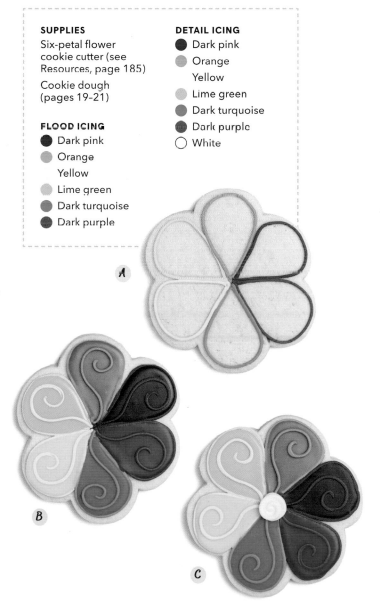

A

B

C

Snow Cone

Y'all this is one of my all-time favorite cookie designs. It is so fun and versatile to make into any colors. Something about the sugar on top makes it so realistic and meta! These would make the cutest platter with some name plaques or "Hello Summer" cookies!

Start by preparing your favorite cookie dough from the options on pages 19 to 21 and cutting out as many snow cone shapes as you would like to decorate! Bake your cookies according to the recipe instructions and let them cool.

Step 1. Outline the paper "cone" part of the snow cone first, using your pale baby blue detail icing. Make the top line of the cone curve slightly downwards. Outline the top ball of the snow cone in white. Allow the outline to dry for at least 30 minutes before moving on to flood. *See A.*

Step 2. Flood the top part of the snow cone first, because it gets dipped in sprinkles. This part is wet on wet, so remember to work quickly and not decorate too many at one time.

Go in rainbow order with your flood icing: dark pink, orange, yellow, lime green, dark turquoise, and dark purple. Start at the left side of the snow cone ball with pink, piping a line along the curve and ending about halfway up the top of the snow cone. Build each color after that, touching the previous color before it, until you reach the right side of the snow cone. While the flood icing is still wet, dip the entire top of the cone into the chunky sugar crystal sprinkles! Okay, now that is adorable, are you seeing it?! *See B.*

Step 3. Flood the bottom of the snow cone in the pale baby blue flood. Allow this to set for at least 4 hours before piping the top details.

Step 4. Using your pale baby blue detail icing, pipe a smooth line along the top of the paper cone. Then pipe scallops under the line. Finish with a tiny heart in the pale baby blue in the center of the cone. *See C.*

SUPPLIES
Snow cone cookie cutter (see Resources, page 185)
Cookie dough (pages 19–21)
White sugar crystal sprinkles

FLOOD ICING
- Pale baby blue
- Dark pink
- Orange
- Yellow
- Lime green
- Dark turquoise
- Dark purple

DETAIL ICING
- Pale baby blue
- White

Funky Flower Heart

This funky design reminds me of henna artwork with the intricate lines and details upon details! This design is perfect for when you are looking to relax by focusing on repetitive shapes and lines. The end result is so stunning you won't even be able to eat them!

I am using my favorite colors . . . RAINBOW! But the best part about these cookies, is, if you don't have the time (or desire) to make these colors, you can simplify and pick just your favorite colors. Or do them all in white or black to create a fancy vibe.

Start by preparing your favorite cookie dough from the options on pages 19 to 21 and cutting out as many heart shapes as you would like to decorate! Mix your heart shapes if you have more than one heart cutter. Chocolate flavor might be a fun one for this if you are giving it for a Valentine's Day gift. Bake your cookies according to the recipe instructions and let them cool.

Step 1. Use your red detail icing to outline the heart around the edge. Allow the outline to set for at least 30 minutes, or until it is dry to a light touch. *See A.*

Step 2. Use the red flood to fill in the cookie completely. Let this dry for 2 to 3 hours, or overnight. The more set up the base icing is, the easier it will be to pipe the details on top!

Step 3. For the rainbow effect, use the colors in rainbow order—or let loose and mix it up however you see fit! Start by drawing a circle about the size of a quarter. I like to draw mine slightly offset from the center, to keep the cookie whimsical. But you could move that center point anywhere you think will look prettiest!

Continued →

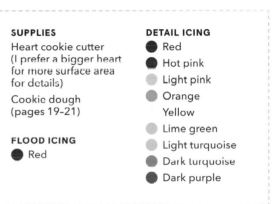

SUPPLIES
Heart cookie cutter
(I prefer a bigger heart
for more surface area
for details)
Cookie dough
(pages 19–21)

FLOOD ICING
● Red

DETAIL ICING
● Red
● Hot pink
● Light pink
● Orange
○ Yellow
● Lime green
● Light turquoise
● Dark turquoise
● Dark purple

A

Step 4. Draw another circle in the next colors, inside the first circle. Pipe tiny dots between both circles. **See B.**

Step 5. Make U-shapes around the outer circle. I can usually fit six to seven Us. The more un-uniform they are, the more whimsical it will look. The more uniform you make them, the more traditional.

Step 6. Make smaller U-shapes inside the Us you just made, again using the next color. **See C.**

Step 7. Starting at the top center of the Us, begin a second round of U-shapes. Be careful to not connect the Us at the base like before: leave a space between them, like petals of a flower between the other petals.

Step 8. Make a fourth set of Us, inside the outer U round. **See D.** In between each outer petal, draw a straight line coming out, then draw a circle line.

Step 9. In your final color, pipe a dot inside each outer circle and then add a tiny heart on the inside of the flower. **See E.**

B

C

D

E

Sunflower & Sunshine!

Here is another one of our favorite multi-use cutters! Both will leave a little sunshine wherever they go! These might be fun to do in a lemon flavor with a lemon glaze, to match the "yellow" feel!

Start by preparing your favorite cookie dough from the options on pages 19 to 21 and cutting out as many sunflower shapes as you would like to decorate! Bake your cookies according to the recipe instructions and let them cool.

Step 1. Outline the outside of the shape in yellow detail icing, following the shape of each petal along the edge. With brown detail icing, pipe a large round center. I like to exaggerate the size here! Allow the outline to set for at least 30 minutes before flooding. *See A.*

Step 2. This step is wet-on-wet sprinkles! Flood the brown center first with your flood icing. While it is still wet, pour the brown sanding sugar over the brown icing. This creates such a shimmery texture! *See B.*

Note: When I am pouring sprinkles like this, I like to do it over a bowl or parchment paper so that I can funnel the excess back into the sprinkle jar. Brush off any extra sanding sugar, so it doesn't get into your yellow flood.

Continued →

SUPPLIES	FLOOD ICING
Sunflower cookie cutter (see Resources, page 185)	● Brown Yellow
Cookie dough (pages 19–21)	DETAIL ICING Yellow
Airbrush and orange airbrush color (optional)	● Brown ○ White
Brown sanding sugar	

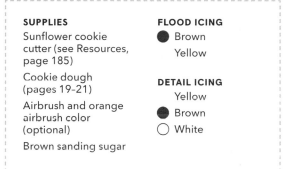

Step 3. Flood the rest of the cookie with your yellow flood icing. Allow the flood to dry for at least 4 hours before moving on.

Step 4. Optional: I love the dimension this step adds to a simple sunflower cookie. Using orange airbrush coloring in your airbrush gun, lightly spray right at the edge of the brown center, working your way outwards on the petals. You want the inside to be dark, golden yellow, fading out to the lighter yellow on the outside. I like to let the airbrush color dry on the cookie for at least 30 minutes before adding any details on top to prevent bleeding colors.

Step 5. Using yellow detail icing, re-outline every petal. I start at the corner of one petal, tracing up the top of the tip, then curving the line back down to the middle of the flower. Do this on every petal, working all the way around the cookie.

Step 6. Use white detail icing to pipe small dots all along the edge of the brown center. That is one beautiful flower! **See C.**

Variation: To turn this cookie into a sunshine, simply substitute the brown center for a pastel yellow. I skip re-tracing the petals, but still do the white dots around the center, and add a cute face to the middle. These would go so cute with a calligraphy plaque "You are my sunshine" cookie! **See D.**

Watermelon Cookie

While it may be simple, this watermelon cookie is one of the most popular designs we have during summer. Maybe it's the perfect bit of nostalgia mixed with the modern gold accent that makes you want to take a big bite! These would make the perfect pool party tray with a few sunshine cookies (page 165).

Start by preparing your favorite cookie dough from the options on pages 19 to 21 and cutting out as many watermelons as you would like to decorate! Bake your cookies according to the recipe instructions and let them cool.

Step 1. Outline the entire cookie in light pink detail icing. If you are using half of a round cookie cutter, pipe a little bite mark at the top as an extra detail! Let the outline dry for at least 30 minutes. *See A.*

Step 2. Flood the entire cookie with light pink flood icing. Let the flood icing dry for at least 4 hours before moving on to top details.

Step 3. Optional: Using hot pink airbrush color, lightly spray the bottom arch of the watermelon, making it darker at the base, fading up to the top, in a smooth ombre effect. If you don't have an airbrush, you can simply leave the watermelon solid pink! *See B.*

Step 4. Using a tip 10 fitted on your dark green detail icing, pipe a thick line, tracing the bottom edge of the cookie for the rind of the watermelon. Pipe a thin line of light green icing on the top edge of the dark green icing. *See C.*

Step 5. Pipe black teardrop shapes pointing toward the center of the melon, for the seeds. Leave space for one seed.

Step 6. Pipe one seed in ivory detail icing and paint it with the gold luster dust (page 16).

Step 7. Re-outline the bite mark at the top of the cookie in light pink detail icing.

SUPPLIES
Watermelon cookie cutter (OR use a round cookie and cut it in half) (See Resources, page 185)

Cookie dough (pages 19–21)

Airbrush and hot pink airbrush color (optional)

Tip number 10

Gold luster dust and clear alcohol

FLOOD ICING
- Light pink

DETAIL ICING
- Light pink
- Dark green
- Light green
- Black
- Ivory

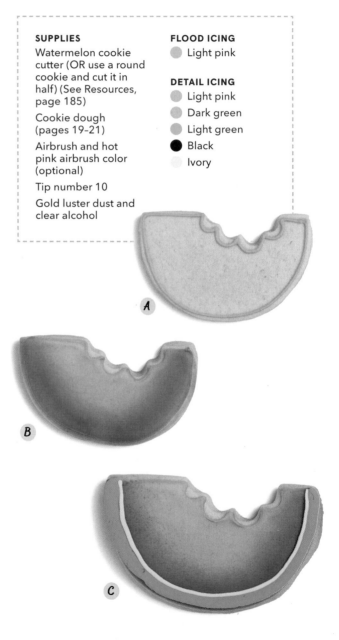

A

B

C

Cool Cookies

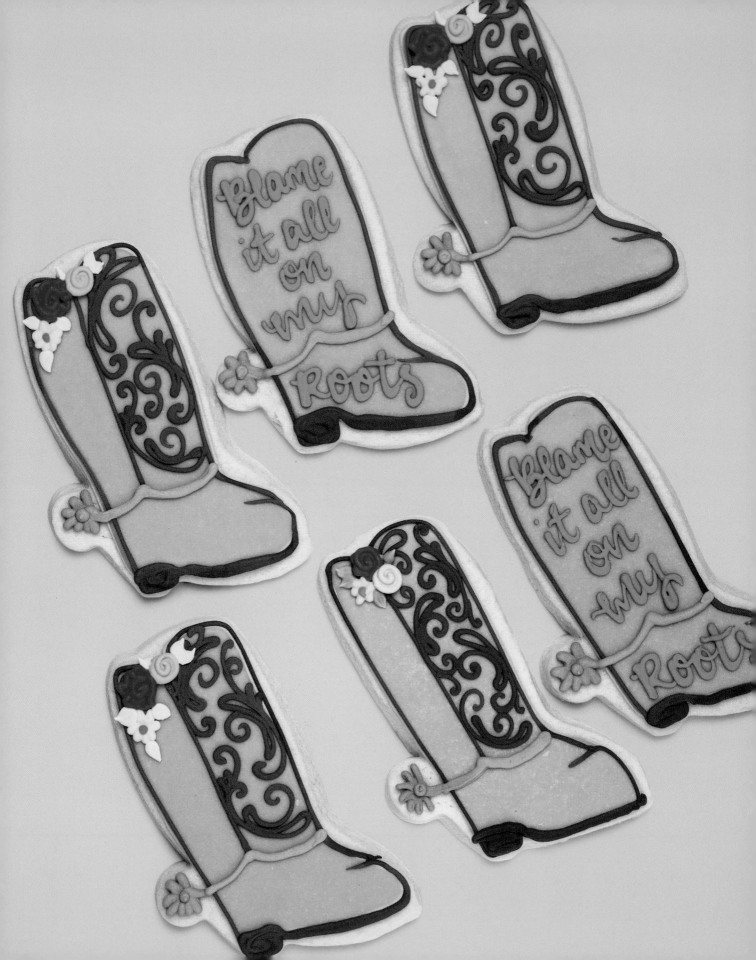

Blame It All on My Roots . . .

I showed up in BOOTS! I couldn't leave this book without at least a nod to my Texas roots. And these cowboy (or cowgirl) boots are my favorite! Jazz them up with floral accents, scroll work, or even a favorite song quote.

Start by preparing your favorite cookie dough from the options on pages 19 to 21 and cutting out as many boot cookies as you would like to decorate! Bake your cookies according to the recipe instructions and let them cool.

Step 1. Using your ivory detail icing, outline the shape of the boot, skipping the spur and heel. Allow outline to dry for at least 30 minutes before moving on. Flood the cookie using your ivory glaze icing. Allow this to set up and dry for at least 4 hours before moving on to top decorations. *See A.*

Step 2. Using your brown detail icing, re-outline the entire shape of the boot. When you get to the heel, follow the shape of the cookie and fill it in brown with the detail icing. Pipe a smooth line for the sole of the boot. I like to add a line going back up the toe to create the "wrinkle" that boots get right there where your toes bend! Go back to the center of the boot and draw a line straight down the middle, ending the line where the spur strap will go.

Step 3. Using your gray detail icing, pipe a spiked spur. Make it almost like a half-starburst shape. Pipe two scalloped lines for the strap across the ankle of the boot. *See B.*

Variations

Add swirls to the front part of the boot in brown detail icing. I use this shape, and just turn it over and under, all different directions, so the boot looks super intricate. Rotate that filigree 45 degrees and pipe it again going up the boot. Then rotate it again and pipe it upside down. I like to add three of our wiggle flowers to the top (page 43). *See C.*

SUPPLIES
Boot cookie cutter (see Resources, page 185)
Cookie dough (pages 19–21)

FLOOD ICING
Ivory

DETAIL ICING
Ivory
Brown
Gray
Colors for details (optional)

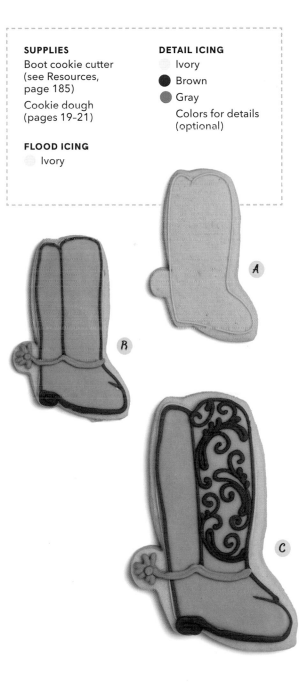

Carved Woodgrain Cookies

Okay, these cookies may look intimidating, but you GOT THIS! They are not as hard as they look, and they have endless possibilities for what you could carve into your "tree." I like using this bigger, fancy plaque shape, because you can fit a lot of shapes on it. This would be super cute to use a heart-shaped cookie with, especially if pairing with a wedding-themed or valentine's cookie set.

Start by preparing your favorite cookie dough from the options on pages 19 to 21 and cutting out as many cookies as you would like to decorate! If you do not have an airbrush or a stencil, you can use a brown food pen, or use brown food coloring and a paintbrush to freehand a woodgrain effect. Bake your cookies according to the recipe instructions and let them cool.

Step 1. Spread a thin layer of brown detail icing on your cookie. Make sure this icing will cover the entire area of your design you will be "cutting out." For this shape I will show you how to make a carved heart! *See A.*

Let this icing set up just enough for the paper you will trace not to stick directly to it, about 30 minutes. If you feel confident enough just sketching directly on the cookie without a paper template, then move on to step 3!

Step 2. Grab a piece of parchment paper and draw the shape you want. Cut it out. You could do initials or a deer silhouette for a fall vibe.

Step 3. Place whatever shape you cut out on the cookie. Using a toothpick, trace lightly around the edge. You can always freehand letters. Just remember you will not be filling in the middle of this design: Err on the side of "too big" for the design, because you can always make it smaller. It is harder to make it bigger without re-smoothing the brown icing underneath.

Continued →

SUPPLIES	FLOOD ICING
Plaque-shape cookie cutter (see Resources, page 185)	Ivory
Cookie dough (pages 19–21)	**DETAIL ICING**
Parchment paper	● Brown
Airbrush	☐ Ivory
Woodgrain stencil	

A

Step 4. Use your ivory detail icing to outline the outside of your cookie shape. Outline the edge of the inner design you traced. For this tutorial, outline the outside of the heart. Allow the outline to set for at least 30 minutes before flooding. *See B.*

Step 5. Using your ivory flood icing, flood the space between the outer edge of the cookie and the outer edge of your heart. Allow this flood icing to set for at least 1 hour, so that when you place the woodgrain stencil on top it will not stick to the icing. If you are not using the airbrush and want to paint or draw the woodgrain effect with food pen or food coloring, let the icing set for at least 8 hours or overnight, until it is hardened.

Step 6. Using the airbrush stenciling technique from page 36, place the woodgrain stencil lightly on top of the cookie. With brown airbrush coloring, lightly spray over the stencil. Follow the same direction as the woodgrain when spraying to prevent overspray and messy edges. *See C.*

B

C

If using food pen or painted food coloring, I like to draw woodgrain by starting with a spiral "swirl" that goes into a straight line. I work around that swirl by adding more lines that arch over and under the swirl, spacing out additional swirls organically, like a wood pattern would look. *See D and E.*

Step 7. If you like the look of your finished cookie, you can leave it as is! Or you can re-outline in ivory or a different color, or even paint the outline gold to make that cut-out shape POP! *See F.*

D

E

F

Fancy WOW Rosette Cookies

You may be wondering what WOW is. Around the bakery, we use that to stand for WET ON WET! And these fancy wet-on-wet designs will leave you saying WOW! I also love to do this design on a heart shape for Mother's Day or on a onesie or rattle for a baby shower!

Start by preparing your favorite cookie dough from the options on pages 19 to 21 and cut out as many plaques or fancy shapes you would like to decorate! Bake your cookies according to the recipe instructions and let them cool.

Step 1. Start by outlining the plaque in a light turquoise detail icing, following the shape of the cookie. Let the outline set up for at least 1 hour before starting the flood process. *See A.*

Step 2. Remember this design is very heavy with detail wet on wet, so work quickly. Do not put too much icing down with the initial turquoise color to prevent any chance of overflow. Start by flooding a thin coat of light turquoise flood icing all over the cookie. *See B.*

Continued →

SUPPLIES
Fancy plaque cookie cutter (or any shape will work!) (see Resources, page 185)
Cookie dough (pages 19–21)
Tip number 4 and number 2

FLOOD ICING
- Light turquoise
- Light pink
- Dark pink
- Lime green

DETAIL ICING
- Light turquoise
- White

A

B

Step 3. Using a tip 4, with your light pink flood icing, pipe random dots all over the cookie. I like to bunch up two or three dots; these will be the roses, so little clusters will look super cute together! *See C.*

Using a tip 2, with your dark pink flood icing, pipe a little swirl on top of each light pink dot. This can be a little messy and that is okay. You will swirl it all together anyway!

Step 4. Use a clean toothpick and gently swirl each dot together. Try to stay shallow in the icing, moving in a circular motion, until each dot resembles a swirled rose flower.

Step 5. Use a tip 2 fitted on your lime green flood and pipe small green dots around each cluster of flowers. Using another clean toothpick, drag the toothpick from the center of the dot outwards, making a leaf shape! Let this flood set up and dry for at least 4 hours before moving on to any top details. *See D.*

Step 6. For this cookie, I am going to write "Best mom ever" because these are perfect for Mother's Day. Follow the template to practice a few times before piping it directly onto the cookie, or just freehand it in your own handwriting! *See E.*

C

D

E

Magical Ombre Heart Cookie

This cookie uses multiple techniques that would look so cute on any shape or design you come up with. The ombre background effect is so trendy and modern. The simple starbursts give a super retro vibe. And the combo is pure magic, no matter what you write on it. These would be so pretty on the strawberry cookie dough recipe. The ombre pink fade makes them the perfect combo!

Start by preparing your favorite cookie dough from the options on pages 19 to 21 and cutting out as many hearts as you would like to decorate! Bake your cookies according to the recipe instructions and let them cool.

Step 1. Outline the entire heart in your light pink detail icing. Allow outline to dry for at least 30 minutes before flooding. *See A.* Flood the cookie with light pink glaze. Allow the cookie to dry for at least 4 hours. *See B.*

Continued →

SUPPLIES	FLOOD ICING
Heart cookie cutter (see Resources, page 185)	● Light pink
Cookie dough (pages 19–21)	**DETAIL ICING**
Airbrush and hot pink airbrush color	● Light pink
Gold luster dust and clear alcohol	○ White
	● Mint
	● Light purple
	● Ivory

Step 2. Using your airbrush, add your pink airbrush color. Slowly airbrush the heart, starting at the top of the cookie and working your way down, making the top heavier in color and fading slowly down. After airbrushing something like this, I like to let it dry for about 30 minutes, to make sure the airbrush color will not absorb into the royal icing I pipe on top. **See C.**

Step 3. From here, you can write whatever you want! Here is a cute example we love for a miscellaneous treat! Using mint detail icing, write "YOU ARE" in a tall skinny font. Practice using the parchment tracing technique we demonstrate on page 173. Or if you have a projector, simply take a photo of the template and trace it onto the cookie using your projector.

Step 4. Using ivory detail icing, write "magic" in a scripty cursive font. **See D.** After the ivory has dried for about 1 hour, you can paint gold over the ivory. (See page 16 for instructions about how to paint gold on cookies.)

Step 5. I like to add extra details by piping tiny mod stars with white detail icing, randomly around the cookie, with tiny white dots for details! I can't wait to see what YOU write on your ombre cookies! **See E.**

C

D

E

Watercolor Cactus

This cactus shape can be SO versatile for many celebrations. These cookies are stand-alone adorable, but wouldn't it be the cutest valentine's pun to pair it with a calligraphy cookie like "stuck on you" or maybe even "free hugs" for the salty valentine in your life?!! Plus, bonus if you don't feel like mixing a ton of different icing colors: these cookies will work up quick because, shocker, you *only* need white icing to make this happen!!

Start by preparing your favorite cookie dough from the options on pages 19 to 21 and cutting out as many cactus shapes as you would like to decorate! I'm using my favorite chubby cactus cutter, but if you want to do skinny cacti, I won't judge ya! Bake your cookies according to the recipe instructions and let them cool.

Step 1. Start by outlining the shape of your cactus in white detail icing. Allow the outline to set for at least 30 minutes before flooding. *See A.*

Step 2. Flood the entire cookie white, using your flood icing. Allow the base icing to dry for 4 hours or more, until you can touch the icing and it doesn't stick to your finger. *See B.*

Step 3. Put a drop of forest green food coloring in your paint palette. Pour a few drops of clear alcohol into the palette. I like to pour a few extra empty palette spaces with just alcohol to make it easier to mix different shades of the green.

Continued →

SUPPLIES

Cactus cookie cutter (see Resources, page 185)

Cookie dough (pages 19–21)

Forest green food coloring

Painter's palette

Paintbrush

Clear alcohol

White nonpareil sprinkles (optional)

FLOOD ICING
○ White

DETAIL ICING
○ White

A

B

Step 4. When you paint on the cookie, the more food coloring gel you get on your brush, the deeper the shade of green will be. You want to get a variety of shades of green. I like to start with a fairly concentrated amount of food coloring on my brush. You can always add more alcohol onto your paintbrush and spread it around. Make an abstract "blob" shape on the cookie, anywhere you would like. **See C.**

Step 5. Add different shapes, building on the original food coloring blob. **See D.** Adding more alcohol will make the watercolor effect grow and branch out on its own all over the cookie. Continue painting the cookie with more or less food coloring, as you want different spots on the cookie to have deeper greens than others. **See E.**

Step 6. Once the cookie is painted, allow it to dry. This could take a few hours or even overnight, depending on how much alcohol you used.

C

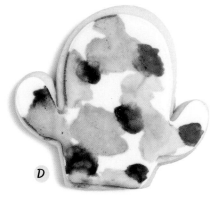

D

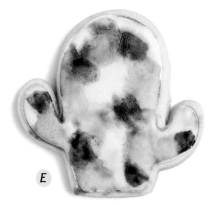

E

Step 7. Optional: If you love the way your watercolor looks, then leave it and love it! To add more details, or if it needs a little cleaning up, start with your white detail icing. Re-outline the shape of the cactus. Then add lines starting from the bottom, reaching to the top middle of the cactus. **See F.**

Step 8. To add even more texture, sprinkle white nonpareil sprinkles over the cookie while your lines are still wet to create the cactus prickles!

F

Resources

All decorating supplies can be found on our website: hayleycakesandcookies.com. Just click over to the "Shop Online" tab and you'll find a whole section of products. We stock tons of sprinkles, bottles, tips, bags, and many of the cutters you need to decorate the magical cookies in this book!

If the cookie cutter design you're looking for is not specifically listed for one of the companies below, you can find it on our website.

Shey B Designs
www.sheyb.com
SheyB creates custom stencils and cutters, with new releases EVERY week! You can also find tons of fancy plaques and basic shapes. I love checking in for inspiration on new designs, including:
Lollipop Ghost (page 145)
Snowy Penguin (page 71)
Stacks on Stacks on Stacks (page 148)
Sunflower and Sunshine (page 165)
Unicorn (page 73)
Whimsy Coffee Mug (page 95)

That's a Nice Cookie Cutter
www.thatsanicecookiecutter.com
That's a nice cookie cutter makes unique cutters and stencils. They will work with you on creating custom designs and shapes as well. I sourced these cutters and stencils from them:
Abe Lincoln Stencil (page 32)
Egg & Bacon (page 85)
Dia de los Muertos Sugar Skull Cookie and Heart Stencil (page 137)
Paulette Bear (page 57)

Kaleidacuts
www.kaleidacuts.com/
This company sells hand illustrated cookie cutters, including:
Peace Sign Turkey (page 65)

Etsy
www.etsy.com
Search for cookie cutters on this popular craft and DIY site. You never know what you'll find!

Truly Mad Plastics
www.trulymadplastics.com
The last time I checked, this company had over 5,000 cutters for sale.

Lettering templates

BRUNCH
buddies

Cheers!

HOME
Sweet
HOME

THANKFUL
Grateful
blessed

I MISS THE
Shell
OUTTA YOU!

I LOVE YOU
beary
MUCH

FEED ME
and tell me
I'M PRETTY

MERRY
Christmas

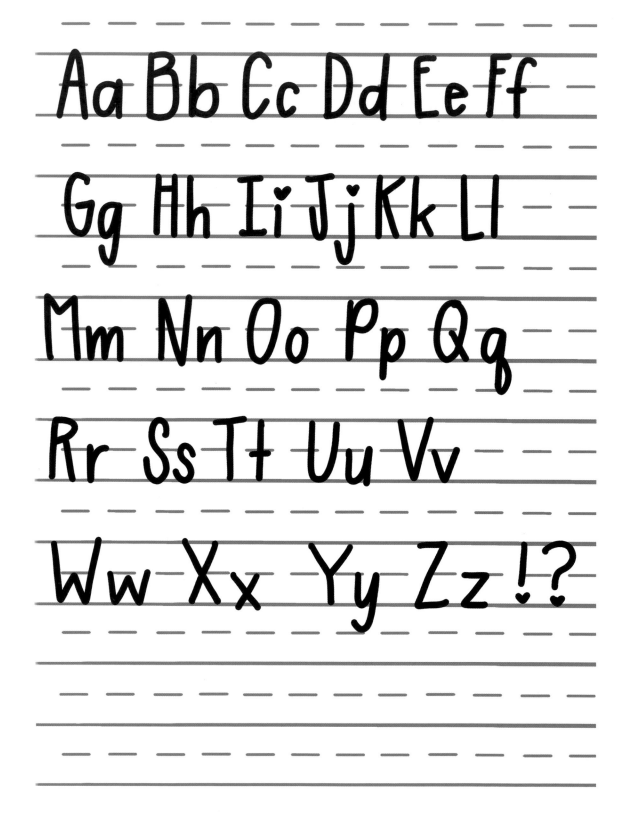

Aa Bb Cc Dd Ee Ff
Gg Hh Ii Jj Kk Ll
Mm Nn Oo Pp Qq
Rr Ss Tt Uu Vv
Ww Xx Yy Zz !?

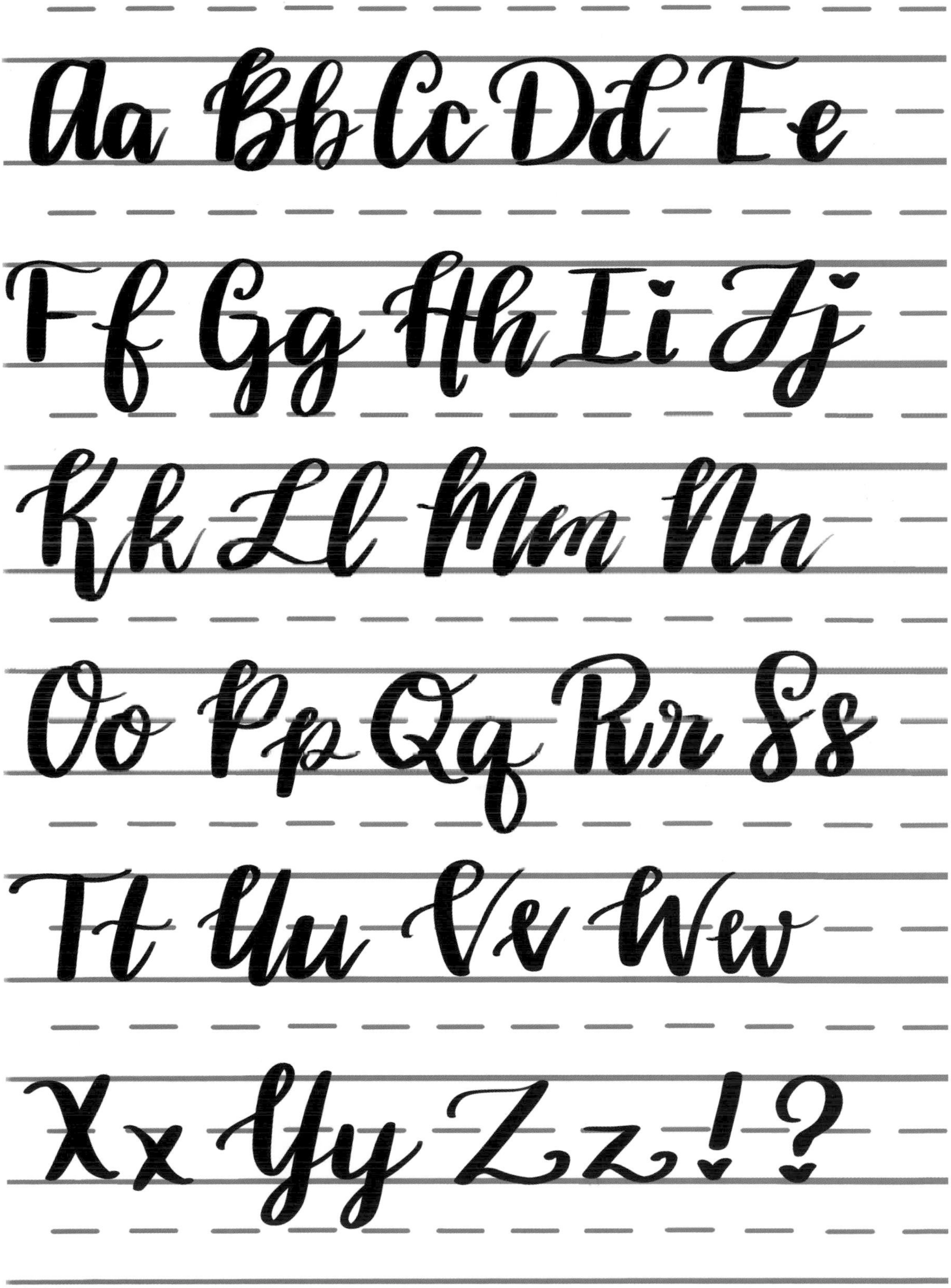

Aa Bb Cc Dd Ee

Ff Gg Hh Ii Jj

Kk Ll Mm Nn

Oo Pp Qq Rr Ss

Tt Uu Vv Ww

Xx Yy Zz !?

Acknowledgments

Thank you to my husband, Mason, for always supporting me; to my brothers and their wives for coming to my rescue any time of day or night; to my mom and dad for putting up with all my procrastination; and to my right hand, Lisa Hammann, for always having my back.

About the Author

Hayley Callaway started Hayley Cakes and Cookies in high school, creating baked goods for her teachers and friends. After finishing college, she doubled down on the business. Her unique cookies, with jokes, memes, and funny ideas that made people laugh, launched Hayley Cakes and Cookies from a local business to a nationwide viral success story. The same year she opened her first brick and mortar location in Austin, Texas, she was featured on Buzzfeed and a few other popular sites. By the next year, the business had more than doubled and she was featured on *Good Morning America*, Food Network, *The Kelly Clarkson Show*, and more. Hayley's bakery has continued to grow, now with multiple locations. Find her online as @thehayleycakes on Instagram or visit her site: hayleycakesandcookies.com.

Index